The Devil on My Doorstep

By Laurie Ann Campbell
and Carol Joan Campbell

PublishAmerica
Baltimore

First printing

PublishAmerica has allowed this work to remain exactly as the author intended, verbatim, without editorial input.

ISBN: 978-1-4489-9325-3
PUBLISHED BY PUBLISHAMERICA, LLLP
www.publishamerica.com
Baltimore

Printed in the United States of America

And if the cloud bursts, thunder in your ear
You shout and no one seems to hear
And if the band you're in starts playing different tunes
I'll see you on the dark side of the moon.

PINK FLOYD

Table of Contents

The Devil
on My Doorstep

Chapter 1

The Format to Follow

Laurie's View

This book will describe two sides of a mental breakdown that I went through. The portions which are shown in this style printing are my views and feelings while my mind was playing cruel tricks on me. The other, italic print portions are the thoughts of my mother depicting the feelings that she was going through as she observed what was happening to me, and how she lived through the experience and proceeded to find help for me and learned how to cope with all of the situations herself.

I wish to bring out that during all of this, the closeness of my mother and myself gave me a firm handle to grasp and pull me through this ordeal, and by living through this hell together, we became even closer and found greater understanding of one another.

I also want to expand on events after the "clinical healing" that went on for a great deal of time, but made the "soul healing" complete and lasting, to give me greater insights of understanding in many areas of life and living. A very important part of the healing was to know how God was always there for me, and without Him, I may have slipped into the power of the demon who seemed to be inside of me. My faith in Him sustained me at all times, and as I slipped further from reality, it was God's love for me and love from my family that pulled me out of the cesspool of evil thoughts that blurred my mind and brought me to the reality of showing God my love for Him.

I hope to show that the process of healing from a severe mental breakdown is a slow one—not accomplished in weeks, or months, but often in years. However, it is possible to live through such an experience and not just get back to "normal", but to become a stronger, more sensitive and loving person, able to cope with any situation and to be a help to others.

Mental health is an area that does not have uniform symptoms, cures or methods of treatment. People still have fears as to how to deal with persons who are suffering with mental illness—perhaps because they realize how vulnerable they may be to going through the same things themselves. Also, unfortunately, they still feel that it is a thing to be hidden and not spoken of or acknowledged.

As difficult as it is to relive and revive my feelings while I was going through such a traumatic period of my life, I truly feel that if persons who are experiencing such times may see that although the struggle may seem horrendous at the time, life can go on and prove to be wonderful and beautiful.

3 B—*Carol's View*

As Laurie regained her true self once more after struggling through such an episode of mental illness, we began to think about writing our thoughts down, to show how this affected her, our family and myself. What she went through was a terrifying experience—one that we had no idea how to stop or where to find help along the way. Granted, now, 30+ years later it is said they have made great progress in dealing with all of this, but talking to others who are experiencing similar episodes, I'm not sure that issues have been fully solved.

I am a saver, and I found that I had saved all of the papers that Laurie had been writing while she was in college and going through all of this mental turmoil. The poems and many of her feelings stated in this book were actually written down at that time. (She had always been a journal keeper, as was I.)

It was difficult to bring all of our memories to the surface—having spent years actually trying to forget them, but remembering and facing feelings brought new healing. Knowing that no matter what had gone on, Laurie's and our faith in God and the true love of family combined with that faith could raise all of us up, victorious over no matter what may have tried to tear us apart.

A person having a breakdown loses reality, and doesn't know where to go to find it again, thus making it imperative that someone who loves them can hopefully guide them towards finding help and being there for them showing love and acceptance while they struggle through the search to once again find their true self, only perhaps this time with greater assurance that they can once again live a normal, healthy, happy life. This is why we have written this book.

Perhaps if you are a family of someone going through a breakdown, you may find some greater understanding of what your loved one is going through and how they feel by reading Laurie's portion of the book. Perhaps you will relate with us as to the difficulties you may encounter while trying to find the right kind of help for the one you love, but not to give up, for there is the right kind of help available somewhere, if you keep on searching.

Finally, if you are a person who has gone through a breakdown, perhaps you will receive some encouragement that no matter what terrible things you have encountered, there is hope that you can get through all of these times and emerge as an even stronger person, able to deal with whatever situations may arise. Always remember that you have fought the good fight and have become the survivor and can remain victorious through the rest of your life—knowing that Faith, Hope and Love will always be with you.

Chapter 2
The Attack

The hate coming from the depth of her soul changed her beautiful blue eyes to squinting dark beads, literally projecting poison towards me—the hated one. She no longer knew me as her mother—I was the Devil and she was out to destroy me. Each time I passed by her, she averted her eyes and turned away. The chanting in her strange, unintelligible tongue grew louder, and my own painful feeling of terror and fright welled up within me. "Laurie, I pleaded, Laurie, don't do that." That seemed to agitate her more, and now, using words I barely understood, she said something about my finding answers in the book. These moments are hazy—the weeks had been long and strained and they finally took their toll. I walked to the piano and picked up a hymnal—the music of the church. "Are the answers here"? My voice rose—filled with choked back tears.

How much more pain was I to endure? This woman who claimed to be my Mother. I would win! I would hold out! She put on such a good show. She may have had the world in her grasp, but the evil that she stood for could not win. She wasn't my mother. She was the continuance of a suffering world. A world bound by sin. She would continue to try to be all powerful—the evil seed. I would not play her game. It was evil, it was insanity. I would not give up, I would survive. Ym dog, ym dog, yhw sah uoht nekasrof em? Enough—enough.

Then she got out of the chair—the recliner in which she practically lived now, and if I thought that I had seen looks of hatred before, now I was literally frozen in terror.

She attacked me!!! I was taken by surprise and lost my defenses immediately—I didn't want to hurt her, but she definitely planned on hurting me and was succeeding. By now she had me pinned down on the floor—her hands around my throat. I was struggling violently—I weigh almost twice as much as she, but her power and strength were unbelievable. I honestly could not get away. As her fingers pressed harder around my throat, I twisted my head back and forth, now crying and shouting— "No, Laurie, No—don't do this." We thrashed about on the floor for several minutes—I was mentally devastated and physically hurting. Finally, my sheer power began to endure, and her weakened abilities let down and I broke away from her and got up, as did she. I stood there, next to the back door and almost transfixed, watched in horror as she calmly walked over to the fireplace and picked up the poker, turned, and with it in her hand, started walking towards me.

I picked up the fireplace poker to go after my mother. I had no feelings of love anymore. Could I really have gone after her with intent to harm or even kill her? How far could I have gone? A memory I do not like to replay. How frightening to have your own flesh and blood turn on you, but the memory of that day had no emotions attached to it.

My moment of horror was quickly surpassed by one of sensibility, and I opened the door and ran outside and then across the street to a neighbor's house—one who knew that Laurie had been having problems. As she opened the door, I entered, crying and said "It's Laurie, I've got to use your phone." I dialed the police to explain the situation and ask for help, rather jerkily—trying to hold back more tears, and they said they would send someone out immediately. My neighbor saw that I was bleeding by my ear, and washed it with a cool cloth. I then called our church and asked for the minister. I had talked to him previously, telling him about Laurie's problems, and he had talked to her also. I knew he couldn't do anything at the moment, but I had to tell him what was happening and to hear his comforting voice.

Then, in just a few minutes, the police officer arrived at my neighbors door. I again briefed him on the situation, and we came back to our house. Laurie had locked the door, but I had a key at another neighbors, and I went over and got it. We opened the front door. Laurie was still downstairs in the family room where our drama had taken place. The officer called to her, but she wouldn't answer at first. Finally she responded with a "Hello" and we cautiously proceeded downstairs. She was sitting calmly on the hearth. I had followed him downstairs after a few seconds—somewhat worried that the sight of me may trigger her again, but it didn't. He talked very calmly to her, and she responded in a calmer way. It was evident by the looks of the room that we had been in a struggle, and now as she talked, she got up and began straightening up the room. As she picked up the poker from the middle of the floor and replaced it in the proper spot, she quietly said "I certainly wasn't going to hurt anyone with this."

I really don't remember what all the officer said to her—mostly just calmly chit chatting—then he told me that perhaps I'd better call our doctor and make arrangements to have her hospitalized, which I did. Our doctor was very shocked when I told him what had happened. He had examined Laurie twice in the last month, and although I had told him that she was having mental problems, he assured me that she was fine. Now he quickly agreed that he would call the hospital immediately and we could bring her right in.

Then the officer called for an ambulance and explained to Laurie that she and I were going to go to the hospital, which she fully agreed to. He suggested that perhaps she may want to pack a few personal items, but she said that wasn't necessary, as she wouldn't be staying—after all, I was the one who needed help.

When the ambulance came—they started to bring out a stretcher, but I assured them that she was calm, and it was not necessary to carry her out. We got into the ambulance—she in back with the paramedics, and I in front with the driver. Again she carried on a quiet, polite conversational exchange all of the way to the hospital.

As I drove away in the ambulance, I remember feeling so far removed from everything. When was this all going to end? I felt nothing—my emotions had shut down long ago. How else could I have attacked my mother? I do remember talking to the paramedics, speaking calmly, just as if nothing had happened. This had all begun three long months ago. Time had stood still. It was now the end of March, maybe help was finally on the way. The end of fright—pain—sleepless nights—hallucinations and nothingness. I needed help, desperately. I needed sleep. God please help me I prayed.

Seated in the admission area of the hospital, I tried to sort everything out. When did all of this really start? What happened to this beautiful person's fragile mind? What had really happened to her at college"? I remember her telling us in the first part of January that she had been really sick for about a week, said she had the flu and that she just hadn't been able to sleep very well.

That was when she had missed the concert.

Chapter 3A

When It Really Began for Laurie

My world had changed. Shattered! It was as if a spell had been cast upon me, as if the door to hell had been opened. I had no control and it was frightening to realize how you are held in fear by the mirrors of your mind. Every observation, every conversation, every logical thought and reason was bounced around and jumbled through every channel of consciousness. All that I could grasp on to was an image of who I had been. It happened that quickly. Where was my soul, my essence, the feeling that told me inside that "I AM"? It was as if the demons of darkness had taken that from me. I felt a black hole inside of my heart. An emptiness. A sadness. My mind was now bombarded with frightening imaginings. I knew people's thoughts and they were all seemingly directed towards me. There was a constant hissing going on. I felt as if I was in a snake pit like in a movie I had once seen. Evil, she is evil, echoed inside my mind.

I tried to remember, days and nights had turned into a blur. Terror gnawed at me constantly. I thought the world had turned against me. Who could help me? Who could try to figure out what was going on in my mind?

I didn't want to be locked up in some mental ward for the rest of my life. That's what they do to crazy people, and that's what was happening to me. I had to find reality again.

I am looking for the happiness that has gone away
I am looking for the innocence that only children seem to know
I am looking for the simplicity that wouldn't stay
I am looking for all my childish beliefs that had to go.
I am looking for the understanding that I need,
I am looking for all the places I haven't seen.
I am looking for the love there used to be—
I am looking for the real me.

I hadn't been in college long, and the first quarter had been such a great experience. What was happening now? I remember that I was supposed to go with friends of mine—we had tickets for a Joni Mitchell Concert and they were going to come and pick me up. I remember waiting for them at the Café next to the dorm. A fellow student came up to me and started talking. I don't remember the exact details. He told me his name was Jeff, and asked what my name was. I told him and then tried to explain to him that I was having problems and that I couldn't think clearly, but I had some friends coming to pick me up. He seemed to realize that I was having a difficult time. He seemed very concerned and said that he would help me. In my mind, I was hoping that this would be the answer to the nightmare that I had been living for the last two weeks. Maybe he could shut off the craziness going on inside of my head. I didn't know how to get a message to my friends, but I went with him. He took me to his home—an old farm house—I remember going upstairs. I tried to tell him my story, about how I had looked through this mirror and had seen all of these faces, and then had ridden my horse and had gone through a battle—good verses evil, and my horse began running and I had no control. I knew it was all an illusion.

It seemed to have begun when I had the flu. I had fainted, and when I woke up, the voices began. I explained that I had been getting some lessons through the mail from a guru who called himself Ram. I had seen an advertisement in a magazine, and they were supposed to raise one's awareness of the present moment. With quiet mindfulness one could reach Nirvana. Each step was supposed to bring one's awareness closer to God and universal love. I told Jeff I had been practicing meditation, but

THE DEVIL ON MY DOORSTEP

now I couldn't stop the voices going on within. Jeff listened patiently, and it was good to be able to say all of these things to him, but I was exhausted.

He said "You can lay down if you don't feel well." "I need to sleep", I said, "I haven't been able to sleep."

Tomorrow would be better. I prayed that God would stop the incessant bantering and conversations going on within myself. Why couldn't I stop my thoughts? God, what have I done? What mirror did I go through? Where are you? Help me. Help me.

Your God does not hear you,
Nor miracles perform.
I'll have your soul—
It was mine when you were born.
How can this be?
What has been my sin?
My parents are good.
They are caring and true.
How could my soul be given onto you?

I laid down—perhaps now I could rest my body and my mind. I think I actually fell asleep for an hour or so.

Laurie was meeting friends that evening to attend a concert, but in the early part of the evening, we received a phone call from them and they informed us that they were not able to find her anywhere. They had waited as long as they could at the designated point, had gone to the dormitory to see if she was there, but no one knew where she was.

Concerned and frightened, we wondered where to go next. After making as many contacts as we could think of, we called the campus police. We gave them her description and she was officially listed as missing. We asked that they be on the lookout for her. Now we felt helpless and spent a few miserable hours wondering what may have happened.

I remember Jeff bringing me back to my dorm room. I don't know if he knew that the police had been looking for me. He suggested that I should call my parents and let them know where I was. I told him I would and thanked him. He said that everything would be all right.

I started losing touch again when I was left alone. My mind was like a flood gate left wide open, as if all of God's imagination was going through me at once. I tried meditating. Then I looked at the mirror on my wall and images of friends and people I knew appeared. It must have been the lessons I'd been receiving. I thought, the lessons worked too well—the transcendental meditation must have worked too well. I had opened myself up to more than guides and helpful spirits. My consciousness had been raised too high, and I was afraid that every spirit who wanted to had claimed a piece of my soul. I felt hopeful for a moment—Ram, the teacher who was sending me the lessons would know what to do. I had his address in New York. I called long distance information and was able to get his phone number. I dialed the number—it rang—"Hello"—it was Ram!!! "This is Laurie". I told him what was going on—that I couldn't stop the flood of thoughts and that I couldn't quiet my mind. I was so scared. "I need your help, Ram"—his reply was "I'm sorry, I can't help you."—"but" and he had hung up. That was it!!! It left me with such a feeling of emptiness. He was supposed to be my spiritual guide. If he couldn't help, who would? Oh Jesus, I prayed, help me. Now I needed to hear the voice of someone I really knew would care, I called Mom and Dad.

Chapter 3B

When It Began for Carol

We were so relieved to hear from Laurie—my husband talked very calmly to her for a while and then he told her to stay right in her room, and that he would be there as soon as he could. I had to stay home with my younger son, but the time seemed to pass so slowly. I knew she didn't sound very good, but we had no idea of all that she had been going through. It was very late when they finally got home and she looked so tired out. We suggested that she try to sleep. Things would probably look a lot better in the morning, but we did suggest that perhaps she should spend a few days safely at home with us.

I was glad to see mom and dad. I hoped that by being back home I would be free from the cloud of confusion and fright that had been following me around campus. Maybe I could shake this. I had to get a grip on myself. I prayed that my mind would stop conjuring up the imaginations which I was unable to stop.

I had been attending classes at college, but things just got worse—3 weeks extended into months—no nodding off, no relaxed state, no sweet dreams. It was one long nightmare for me. At 18 I did not know how to explain to anyone what was happening or even where to begin. I woke up one morning and seemed not to go back to sleep for 3 months. I couldn't sleep, so I watched television and listened to music day and night. I would play my guitar and strum unknown melodies for hours. I was going longer and longer without any reprieve from the constant barrage in my head. It was getting hard to recognize reality.

I'm lost in confusion,
Life's not meant for me.
I'm hanging by my hopes
And fear they'll never be.
I gave up all desires
And met the devil's face—
To give up love and honor
And lost myself—and grace.
I saw illusions past and present
And screamed inside in fright.
The ever present living nightmare
Going on inside all night.
If I could live again one day
Without the pain I felt—
To remember how to love again—-
I prayed this while I knelt.

I wanted to be able to sleep. To actually wake up in the morning and start out fresh.

Chapter 4
When the Bough Breaks

Little did we know that the bough was breaking and that the cradle would fall. Laurie was so good at trying to convince everyone that she was fine. The first week-end we brought her home was just a masquerade played by all of us to convince us all that she would be back to normal. We did, however begin the long process to find help for her. We started with the family doctor—telling him on the phone that she was having mental problems, but when we took her to see him, she was her usual sweet, normal sounding self, and of course he found absolutely nothing wrong.

We were trying to dissuade her from going back to college, but she was adamant that she had to be back in school, and of course the doctor fully agreed with her. We were filled with apprehension, but finally gave in and drove her back to her dorm.

Up to this point, I kept telling myself that it would end. Tomorrow would be better, but each night began another sleepless battle. I prayed that

God would stop the incessant bantering and conversations going on. Why wouldn't it stop?

The evil mother to which you were born,
By all mankind has been kindled with scorn.
I have the power and forever I shall reign.
There is no good, for all is pain.
Take this world and all it's shame,

I've found a fool to take the blame.
There are no miracles or saints to save,
No precious blood that God's son gave.

The words were pouring out in my head, but I couldn't give in to it. I couldn't give in to these evil images I was having.

I cannot listen to this blasphemy.
I have committed no sin to thee.
I believe in God and the powers above
For the strongest truth in this world is love.
So fight then—fight until you can only hope
That God will give you strength to cope.
I will go to any length
I will take from you God's mighty strength—
His wisdom and caring and turn them to dust.
For mankind cannot love without lust.
Oh Jesus, help me. What do I do? Help me Mom. Help me Dad.

How do I explain the fear and terror I felt. Nowhere to run, nowhere to hide. It was with me all the time. I grasped onto any remnant of reality—I knew I had to hold on. I couldn't give in, but I didn't know what was wrong. Were demons really tearing down my door? I kept telling myself no, yet the chaos inside of my mind increased. It was as if demons had entered and their eyes took over for mine. They looked inside through me. They could see the madness of human-kind. I heard screams from through the ages. Let me out!! Let there be an end!! There is no hope!! I could feel pain, as if a knife wrenched my stomach, slowly digging deeper. The blade dug in and twisted inside. Darkness had settled in. Would this torture never end? Don't let me go, God. Don't let me go.

My room mate at college didn't really have an idea of what was going on with me. She knew that I was spending most of my time now at a house a couple of miles away from the dorms, but that was about all. There were other students living in the old farm house, and for many days and nights, the farm house kept me away from the rest of the world—a place where

I could battle the storm. I know they tried to help me. They never charged me rent or made me pay for food. There were times when I could reason everything out, and then reality would slip away again.

While staying at the house, I met Ted. He had been gone for a couple of days and I had been using his room to try and sleep. When Jeff introduced us, Ted smiled and I felt comforted. He was handsome, tall, with long brown hair. He had grown up in rural Wisconsin, had logged up north for a few years before deciding to go to school. I guess it still was not that apparent to anyone that I was having problems. He and I spent the evening together. I thought back and wondered, had I met him at a party before? Had he seen me around campus with my friends? Why would he want to be with me and go out with me without knowing who I was? Maybe I had chit-chatted with him at a party and not really paid attention.

We watched TV together that night. Wow, this was the first time I had watched TV since all of this had begun. My mind couldn't handle it. I tried watching and listening, but between my imagination and the regular barrage that is on network TV, I was convinced that the devil had control of the shows that were on.

I tried to concentrate on Ted, as this was our first evening spent together. A nice quiet evening at home. He had popped a big bowl of popcorn to share. I really did want to know him—even more, I wanted someone to help me and hold me because inside I was so scared. He talked and we cuddled. We watched TV for the evening—we watched Saturday Night Live. I was becoming intrigued by the show. I felt drawn into the television, as if this drama was really going on and we were all a part of it.

He had a joint—I had smoked Marijuana in my teen years. It was pretty common back then—remember this was back in the 70's when drinking was socially acceptable and drugs were experimental and intriguing. I was afraid to smoke it because of my mind, but then I figured that I couldn't get any worse than I was. Maybe it would help. Maybe the pot would mellow me out. I took a couple of puffs. He asked if I liked it. "It must be strong," I said. "Yeah, it's good", he said. I can't tell you if it really was or not. Now my imagination was really going. "Hang on Laurie, don't let go, I told myself." I was losing my sense of reality rapidly. The devil was talking to me—laughing at me, because I couldn't handle it. The TV was going and Ted was smiling.

Laurie, you will make it
We're going to take care of you tonight.
Let go, everything's gonna be all right.
Hold on, hold on—
God's got you in His care.
It will take a while—
This is a terrible scare.
Be brave, Just smile.
You are going to make it through the night.
Just believe and hold on tight.

This was a voice that I would come to recognize. A voice I had heard in my younger days. A voice that upon command could quell the storm within and let me know that I would hang in there. There was still love in this world. There was a promise that God was going to get me through all of this. I was glad to be with Ted that night. So I stayed at the old farmhouse. The house became my refuge.

During the day I read the Bible out loud—it made it easier to breath. I was having a hard time breathing—my chest and stomach felt like knives were in it. No sleep brings physical pain, my jaws were clenched— the tenseness was felt throughout my body—my bones ached, my muscles were tight. I hurt all over from total fear and lack of sleep. Reading the Bible brought some relief by renewing my faith which was all I had to fall back on.

After another couple of weeks, we got a phone call from a fellow—Jeff. We never met him, and never had any other contact other than the phone call. He was the one who had taken Laurie into the house. He talked to us about Laurie and truly seemed concerned. He said that his sister had had a mental breakdown, and he was convinced that Laurie was in the process of having one also. He advised us that he felt we should come to school and get her and find some help for her.

We did take his advice, as we truly knew that things were still not right with her. We went to school and found her and convinced her that it would be best if she moved back home with us for a while.

I was surprised to see my Mom and Dad at school I hardly remember what they really said to me other than they wanted me to move back home for a while. Somehow I guess that I wanted to do just that—I was too tired to protest and too frightened to do anything but be happy to be with them. Perhaps the safety of home would be good for me. I watched as they packed up all of my belongings, and willingly headed back to what I hoped would be security and happiness.

She did seem to be better when she came back this time, and her younger brother seemed so happy to see her. He could always seem to relate to her with no problem at all. Perhaps time and our love would help eventually.

There was too much life ahead of me. Dreams to reach. Goals to make. I'm just 18—make me strong. Don't let me go down. I constantly reminded myself, "You will survive". Still, each day was longer—each night without restful sleep was more terrifying. My thoughts were by now more than just confused, reality was hard to hold on to. I was everything that falls into the lines of mental illness. Paranoia, grandiose delusions, hallucinations. By the middle of February, my hopes had failed. I read the Bible. I feared that I was forever doomed to this, and the Bible became my only grip with reality. There had to be love left in this world. I couldn't end up this way. When would it end? Perhaps there would be no end— perhaps I was eternally damned.

Chapter 5
A Quandry—What to Do

Now we were presented with a new problem—Bill and I were scheduled to attend a business trip to Jamaica. What should we do? It was just for a few days but was Laurie capable of not just staying alone, but taking care of her brother? She was always good with him, and seemed calm and took time to talk to him. At age eighteen she had certainly always been able to take care of him, in fact she was like his second mother. He was only ten then, and I'm not sure exactly how much he realized what all was going on with her. We certainly couldn't bring someone in to take care of her—that would have never gone over. If only her older brother were here. He was in the Navy at this time. She always looked up to him so much, and we would have had no qualms then, but we had to make a decision.

Finally we decided to go, making secret arrangements with several close friends who knew our concern about Laurie, to come over for some reason that would make sense to her as legitimate, but ultimately to check up and see that everything was OK. Her brother was in school during each day, so it was afternoons and evenings that we were concerned about. Finally we talked to him and informed him that if anything came up that frightened him about Laurie he was immediately to go over to our trusted neighbors house, and she had instructions then to call my sisters for help.

Well, after 3 days in Jamaica, which were filled with anxiety, and checking at the front desk for messages every few hours, we got home—to an empty house. Our son had ended up going over for help and both he and Laurie were safe at my sister's home. Of course we immediately went over to get them. I still am not sure exactly what happened at that time. I guess things progressed too rapidly after that.

Apparently she had calmed down after she was at my sisters, and it had only been for a day. They had decided not to contact us in Jamaica as they knew we would be home so soon. Bless the family for being there for her and our son. She seemed glad to see us, and certainly our son was, so we went back home, again not knowing just what to do, just anxious to be able to at least get him back to school and with his friends. Another couple of days went by, but they were not good ones for Laurie or for us. Then came the day when things finally came to a head, I had the confrontation with her, and then came the attack.

I was determined that all that was evil would be conquered. If this was the devil, I would win. If there was a God of love, I would hold out. My mind had gone from January to March from disoriented to psychotic. I couldn't slow down my thought processes. Each 24 hour period of non-stop thinking had brought a next day of wild imagination. Imagination that had no purpose but to win over evil. Sadly it was my mother that seemed at that time to represent all evil. The mother of all sin. She had all power over me. Where could I go? To New York and see if I could find Ram and plead with him to help me? All I knew of Laurie was a remembrance deep inside. A soul that I had to fight for—a soul that had been mine. I wouldn't give up, but who could help me? Too much time had gone by. My grasp of reality was so frighteningly behind the realm of reason, all I could do was to continue on with the drama playing inside of my head. I would survive!!!

No, you should be damned. I'll take the world because of you.
I want your soul—give it to me.
God, I can't give up. Why won't this stop?
This evil woman is at me again.
The Devil cannot win, let me go—let me go.
I want you now—you will not win!
I have you and all that you can give,
No good shall save you.

I will not listen, I won't give in. I will fight this battle. I will win, in the name of God I will win. And so I attacked.

As described in the first few pages of this book, the attack happened, and we ended up at the hospital.

Finally I had Laurie registered and up in the mental health unit. I had called my husband, and by then he had arrived. I didn't see her again before I left that afternoon, but as I walked towards the elevator, I felt, with a sense of guilt, the biggest feeling of relief that I had felt in months. Finally we had found a way to help Laurie. Finally someone actually listened to us, and if it took blood still running down behind my ear, and deep bruise marks around my throat, it was worth it. Now others admitted that the help we had pleaded for in the past few weeks was indeed warranted.

Now it seemed that all we could give her was love. We didn't know how to take care of her physical or mental needs. We couldn't simply put our arms around her and protect her from aches and pains and danger as we had been able to do all through her life. My baby! My angel! To see her hurting so, but no, it wasn't her. What had happened? We had to hand her well being over to strangers, but we knew that God was ultimately in charge, and we all had faith that He would take over, so we just put our trust in Him and enveloped her in our love and prayers.

Chapter 6
The Clinical Healing

While Laurie was in the hospital, the first action taken was with drugs for sedation, which finally brought her rest—she hadn't slept through nights for weeks. That's about all she did now for the first few days. I wasn't even sure at first if she would want to see me or not. I was truthfully frightened that the sight of me would once again set her off, as I seemed to always represent the evil one to her. Her father was the first to see her—she always seemed to respond to him more readily than she would to me. She seemed to be doing so much better, even after just a few days, and she received me seemingly quite well.

After she had been hospitalized for a week, we brought her home for the weekend. She seemed pretty good for the first day, but towards the time that we were to bring her back to the hospital on Sunday, she began to be irrational again, and started "preaching" to me and once again seemed to indicate that I was an evil element. Once again I had the feeling of relief to get her back to the hospital, which filled me with terrible feelings of guilt again. Her progress in the next few days seemed to go better, and by now she had gotten to know a few other persons in the ward and at least was getting well rested and was eating good.

Thank heavens the hospital that we took her to was not a locked ward—not sure if I could have put her behind locked doors that would act like a cage. Also, it was fully assured to us that no shock treatments would ever be administered at this establishment, which made us a bit more confident that nothing drastic could be done without our permission.

The biggest problem that we had at this time was the fact that no one would acknowledge my husband and I as being responsible for Laurie. She was eighteen, and as far as society and everyone else was concerned, this meant that we suddenly seemed to fade into the background. The psychiatrist would talk to me briefly over the phone but would not agree to meet with us, as he felt that it had no bearing. Laurie seemed to be the only one who he would consider, whether she seemed competent or not. We did have a meeting with the nurses on the floor, and they were as informative as they could be, but somehow we resented that our request for a meeting with the doctor was ignored.

I was finally hospitalized, which was anguish to my parents, but even more it was a relief. I was in the hospital for 2 weeks, given some sedatives and an anti-psychotic drug. Everything seemed fine. Wow, it was pretty amazing. However, things did not just go back to normal for me. The experience definitely changed me and had an effect upon me. For one thing I no longer felt my emotions. They were empty. There was a void. I did not feel any anger, nor did I feel any joy or any fear, and I did not know how to explain all of this to anyone. I couldn't and I wouldn't cry.

I don't believe that anyone else came to visit Laurie while she was in the hospital those two weeks, except for our minister. As it turned out another woman from our congregation was in the same ward at the same time, so we could joke a bit about having our own congregational meeting on the floor. He did go to see her a couple of times.

No one really knows how to handle a situation with a mental patient. Even our own families didn't know if they should call her or have contact with her or just what to do. They certainly wouldn't have hesitated to visit her if she was suffering a physical problem. Of course I certainly couldn't blame them—we were just as confused. People seem to think that a mental patient is suddenly incapable of making any decisions and seem to lose trust in their abilities of thinking at all.

This was the first step in the basic clinical healing, but there were so many more steps to go—a journey in life that none of us ever anticipated would happen, but with God's guidance, we continued on together, stepping carefully, following an unfamiliar path, but all of us traveling back hand in hand to the lives that we had known before she had the breakdown.

1 Corinthians: chapter 13, vs. 12 & 13

For now we see in a mirror dimly, but then face to face. Now I know in part; then I shall understand fully, even as I have been fully understood. So faith, hope, love abide, these three, but the greatest of these is love.

Chapter 7
The Long Road Back to Recovery

When Laurie was finally home from the hospital, a new phase of recovery began. We all lived under a feeling of rejoicing for the "recovery of reality", but with a feeling of apprehension and fear of what may possibly cause a relapse or trigger a bad response. We weighed our words carefully, not wanting to anger or trouble her. I still felt as if I was the bad one in her eyes, so even if I felt I had a good suggestion, I seldom said it to her. Instead I would tell my husband, and he then would make the approach and suggest it. She seemed to be more receptive to it if it came from him.

She still spent a great deal of time just sitting, but now just looking more contemplative rather than angry. She still responded well to her younger brother, and that was comforting. At this time she didn't have much to do with her old friends

Rumors had sped quickly that I had "flipped out." A couple of friends continued to call, but I became pretty depressed after I was out of the hospital. I felt as if my personality was completely gone. I had no soul—that spirit that shines inside of you. It was gone. I had no emotions left. I knew I had to do things, but I just didn't know quite what those things should be. I didn't really blame my friends for not coming around, and I knew that I could never explain to them what had happened without pushing them away further, as the whole thing was so bizarre. I didn't think they'd even believe me.

The healing was not overnight. I had developed an eating disorder through the ordeal, much to my dismay. I had always been quite conscious of my weight. Being quite chunky by the sixth grade, the school nurse offered her help and took the time each week to weigh me in. I worked hard to make better food choices, saying no to the extra cookies and chocolate that I adored. My dog enjoyed our daily walks and it made for easy exercise. I was able to lose twenty pounds and grew several inches taller at the same time. The pounds stayed off during my teen-age years and I was able to fit into fashionable junior sizes and felt more confident about myself.

Now, not being able to control my impulses to eat was alarming. The fear of gaining weight was even more alarming.

My lack of control caused me great shame and guilt. Not much was known about bulimia at that time. I had no idea why I was going through this. What was wrong with me now? I struggled with a double life. I was too ashamed to let anyone know. The thought of food and eating consumed me. This led to depression. I desperately wanted to prove to myself that I was normal, so I spoke to no one about this and kept it secret. I would take long hikes to keep me moving and hoping to drive away the temptation to consume more food. At least if I wasn't in the house, I did not have access to the refrigerator or the pantry.

Now came another difficult period of time. Laurie was back to reality, but not quite ready to get back into a daily work routine or ready to be living on her own. What was the next step?

I called the Psychiatrist that had seen Laurie at the hospital and tried to explain what was going on and that she really wasn't herself as yet, but he maintained that she was fine. How could he possibly even make a statement like that? He knew her for two weeks, the first few days being out of her head. We had known her for eighteen years, but our opinion didn't seem to count at all. I asked again if I could meet with him, but he refused and said that everything had to be up to Laurie.

I had my old memories back. I could remember what my personality had been like before the breakdown. That became my challenge—to become the person I knew I had been and have feelings again. I loved my mother and father but it was more like a baby's love—out of need. I wanted to be able to really feel the emotions of love that I used to have for both of them.

I of course kept searching for help. I finally, through our County Mental Health Association heard of a Psychologist who held group meetings at the same hospital where Laurie had been treated. I called him and was favorably impressed by our conversation. At this point in time I had learned the "correct" terms to use asking him if it was a "threatening" or "non-threatening" situation. (Sort of the difference between preaching or listening). He assured me that it was a completely "non-threatening" situation. I then explained Laurie's situation at this time and asked if she would be able to join his sessions, and he agreed. Of course by this time I was leery also, so I asked if he would meet with Laurie and if my husband could come with and he replied" certainly, that would be fine." Finally someone who would acknowledge that we were her parents and a part of this whole situation.

The next week Laurie and Bill met with this wonderful (former minister) psychologist. I will never forget that day—they came home from the session, and when Laurie walked in the door, she had a genuine smile on her face and a sparkle in her eyes. My heart rejoiced as I looked at her and finally thought "I have my Laurie back".

When Mom and Dad first suggested the group sessions, I was willing to try, after all I had found that when we had similar sessions in the hospital, it did seem to help me open up more. I felt comfortable knowing that Dad would be going with me to meet this Psychologist and perhaps I might even find out a little more about other people who were having problems also.

After meeting with the group for several sessions, Laurie seemed more confident, and better able to relate to people. I feel it was good for her to find that others had been going through similar situations and had the same struggles getting back into everyday living just as she had been going through.

Having tried out the group sessions was a good experience. When I was in the hospital, the group sessions there had offered support and compassion towards one another. The awareness of what the other patients were going through did help me to cope better with all I had gone through. We were supportive of one another. Each offered encouragement and wished me well upon my release. They understood me it seemed, but would others I had wondered?

Laurie didn't really tell us much about the group sessions, just a few comments about how many there were there, etc. She intimated that many of them had gone through things like she had, and perhaps that made her feel more comfortable just to be able to talk about them. We could see that the sessions were having a positive impact on her and she seemed to have an increase in happy times, so it definitely was accomplishing something.

As the weeks went by, I began to feel fairly comfortable not just listening to others in the group, but actually sharing things and then listening to their input about it. I guess I even felt my confidence growing that maybe I really was doing OK. I really did like Dr. Jay—he had a calm, soothing voice and never seemed shocked at anyone's comments about what they had gone through and how they reacted to things. I heard lots of stories, and began to think that the problems I'd had weren't as terrible or frightening as some of them had experienced. The more I spoke up and shared things, the more I built up confidence in myself and in my future. I wasn't feeling shame for things. I actually began to wonder if I couldn't just make it on my own without relying on opinions of others. Perhaps I was really making progress. I looked forward to the weekly sessions. As a group, we offered input for each other and gave our evaluations of the progress that was being made.

Laurie had told us that the group had input on when they could be done with the group. Finally it was her time—she came home and informed us that her meetings were over—the group all voted that it was time for her to move on and made her feel confident that she could keep going forward emotionally, and get back to her life as it had been before and work to achieve a happy future. Now I really felt that the next step had to be helping her get back to independent living—holding a job—moving on with her life. This was the ultimate goal for both of us, but it still had to be done carefully, without breaking the ties completely in just one swoop.

I called one organization known to help in various situations and asked if they had any rather "supervised" living places that might be her answer. They stated that they did, but we probably couldn't afford them. When I asked what she meant, she replied that only people who were on welfare could afford the prices charged. I certainly felt good about that!!!!!! Just what a person needs to hear.

We felt that as Spring vacation was coming up, it may just be beneficial to the whole family to spend some time together and do a bit of traveling.

My family decided to take a vacation over the spring break to visit some relatives. We drove to Detroit. We did a lot of sight-seeing along the way visiting such places as Lincoln's birthplace in Springfield

Illinois, a tour of Tony the Tiger at the Kellogg's Cereal factory in Battle Creek and the Ford Museum at Greenfield Village. This was a nice diversion. I was in control of my thoughts now, other than my food problem. I was hopeful. Hopeful that I was on the path of normal again. This would be the first social interactions I had after coming home. I was anxious and a bit nervous. I had been very young the last time we had been together to visit.

As it was, I felt comfortable and relaxed while visiting these relatives. Their hospitality and graciousness instantly put me at ease. My brother and parents were enjoying the time together. We had a grand tour of Detroit, visiting the Renaissance Center that had newly opened, driving over to Windsor and attending a Detroit Pistons basketball game. We returned back home in time to be able to attend the Easter service at our church. The significance to me was being met with songs of joy and singing halleluiahs. The flowers and beautiful music were reminders to me of the promise of my faith. This was the reassurance that salvation was offered and given freely. I had risen from the depths of my hell and been lifted up strong and victorious. The torture of my mind and the madness that held me inside had given way. Darkness did not reign over me. There was hope. My faith had sustained me.

We all had a wonderful time on our trip, and indeed is was a good breather for all of us. Laurie had seemed to do very well and it was good to see her seem to enjoy herself. Again, bless times with family to make us feel welcome and show us such good hospitality.

It was good to get back home again and especially to celebrate Easter in our own church and spend the day with all of our family joined together.

I was anxious to get back to some sort of productive life but I just didn't have any idea of what I wanted to do. Ideally I would have wanted to go back to college, but I did have fears that it may bring on similar episodes that had developed when I was there before. I loved the learning process, and I really wanted more education, but perhaps not college just now. Time to get a job

For two weeks, I was happy flipping burgers. Then a friend of mine recommended Midwest Challenge. They were a Christian based organization with the mission to help teens and young adults that were uncertain of the direction they were going in. I felt this might help me to find a new direction and a chance to be out on my own again.

I packed my bags and headed into the big city—my folks were not too happy about it. The housing was not in a very good part of town at that time.

Bill and I weren't too thrilled with Laurie's decision, but we had never heard any bad things about the organization, so we just had to put faith in the group and hope that it would help her.

We started each day with Prayer and Bible Study at 7:00. We then had breakfast and packed our lunches and we were given our different duties. The jobs were interesting enough—we did bulk mailings. Sorting—posting—packing and shipping. The rules were simple—No Smoking—No Swearing—No Drugs—No Alcohol. The boys had one house, the girls another. While the premise was admirable, it was geared to help those suffering from drug addiction and alcohol abuse. Not my real problem. After two months, I was ready to leave the inner city and told Mom and Dad that I wanted to move back home.

We were happy to have Laurie home again. The experiences hadn't hurt her, but we were glad that she had made the decision that she would be happier somewhere else.

I was glad to get home again in our wooded, suburban setting and back with my family. As good luck would have it, I was able to quickly find a job that I liked, and was fairly content.

Then, one day I was flipping through a magazine and I noticed an ad for a local Travel School, and that appealed to me. This was something that sounded really interesting, and the idea of learning more about travel, which I always thought was wonderful, was quite appealing. I showed it to Mom. She got some more material from the school, and as we both sat down and looked it over I readily agreed that I thought I would like it very much. At last I might really be able to regain my independence, get back into learning, but perhaps not quite as intensive as at college, and I could find a happy and respected career to build my future on.

Finally we found a solution that was a happy one for both Laurie and ourselves. This travel school turned out to be one that my sister had actually attended many years ago, so I knew it was reputable and really did a great deal for their students.

The new session of school was a few weeks away, and we had heard about a trip to the Bighorn Mountains that the young people from our church were planning. We checked and found that they would have room for one more. She had enjoyed the trip to Detroit so much, and we felt she was ready to be on her own and share some special times with the people at church. We offered the plan to Laurie, and she was enthusiastic about her, so yet another trip was planned.

I did decide to take a back packing trip into the Bighorn Mountains that was being offered by our church. I've always appreciated nature and loved hiking. The opportunity to spend some time up in the mountains, away from the city and home was appealing to me. It was something to look forward to and another step forward in forgetting the past events. I had never been involved with the youth church group so it meant all new faces and people to meet. We met together a couple of times to organize and plan the trip. I seemed to fit in alright. I was okay and the group of us departed the day after my nineteenth birthday. What a long year it had been.

We loaded our gear and us into an old yellow chartered school bus. Our fist stop after an eight hour drive overnight was at Wall Drug and then the long drive through the haunting but beautiful Badlands. I had not been through these since I had been seven years old. To revisit this route helped me to relive happy childhood memories of the family trip we had made to the Black Hills.

We drove through the night and the group awoke to see the outline of the mountains with the purple sunrise. Now that the mountains were in sight, the energy stirred through the group, knowing that we would soon be arriving to our destination. It was glorious driving into the mountains leaving the monotony of the Great Plains behind us. We arrived at the rustic log lodge where we slept in cabins for the first night. The smell of the pines, the beauty of the towering trees along with the crispness of the fresh air was invigorating.

We were each given a packet of devotions that we would use for the week. Each psalm was related to the sacred beliefs of the Dakota Plains Indians that had resided in these mountains before the fanatics of greed and ownership killed or drove them away.

So much really goes hand in hand between religions. Both embracing our creator and great spirit, respectful, grateful for the love and abundance that have been offered to us. It is sad that neither beliefs—Christian or Native American are willing to embrace each other. We have lost much of our respect for the beauty of our environment and connectedness with each living creature, which was essential for the American Indians.

These beautiful devotions helped to restore my core beliefs, helping to eliminate the torturous thoughts that had preyed upon me day and night for such a long time.

The next morning we each had our chores to do and geared up. We distributed camping equipment and the food amongst us, along with our clothing and sleeping bag, keeping all to a minimum. We would be out for five days in remote terrain with only the mountains at our side and sky above us. After four hours of hiking we were above the timberline and snow was still present in many places. The water was pure and clean. Clean enough to drink right from the many streams. My thirst was continuously rewarded with a drink. Cold, pure water. The taste which I will perhaps never have a chance to compare with again. Filtered by nature from the highest peaks as it tumbled over the boulders and stones and pebbles along the sandy banks.

Each breath was a cleansing awakening. Fresh, crisp, refreshing. Reviving my senses and awareness. Just as Maria Von Trapp singing in her solitude "I go to the hills when my heart is lonely. I know I will hear what I've heard before..." the mountains offered their reassurance of unchanging strength and fortitude for me.

The week spent with new acquaintances and shared experiences was a great giant step in my healing. Restoring my faith and confidence in myself. I felt assured that I could be with others and feel comfortable in their presence. I felt acceptance from them. My own acceptance of myself was still critical and shadowed. Occasional traces of the voices were close by. Yet I knew that I had control and I was able to let them go. The fear subsided. I left the mountain knowing it would always be there waiting for my return. Its' time imprinted upon my soul. Always a reminder to me of the valleys and the peaks that life holds. You just have to get up and get through each day, one step at a time and you can make it to the top.

When Laurie came home she looked so happy and was excited to tell us about all of her experiences and about all of her new friends. We knew it had been good for her, and now we were all excited to have her launch on yet another journey.

Chapter 8
Threshold of Faith

It was such fun getting Laurie signed up for school—going over to check out the apartment where she would be living, and finally getting her packed up and moving into her new situation. Of course Bill and I both felt some reservations about the whole thing, but we had to have faith that this was the right step forward to open new doors for her. She looked happier than she had for several months, and we were so pleased—we just had to believe that all would go well.

I was excited to finally be back in a school situation. I had always had such a quest for learning, and now I finally had a new opportunity. The whole concept of the school appealed to me. I felt that God was directing this move and knew it would be a good one for me.

I loved the downtown setting and being in an apartment was great. I met new people and made new friends. I was really having fun, and it felt wonderful. I invited my new friends from out of state to come home with me on weekends, and Mom and Dad always treated them so well that they looked forward to spending time at our home. I was once again part of a social circle and felt good about myself.

I called Laurie quite frequently. I could always tell by the tone of her voice how things were going. Mostly, she seemed to be doing very well. Occasionally I felt that she was perhaps a little down and then would talk a little longer, and usually she would seem to spark up again.

She usually came home on weekends, and at times even brought a friend home with her, and we were pleased when she did. She even had more contact with some of her old friends, but mostly it seemed that she had begun to find new friends, and that was OK. She even started dating—a big step.

I was enjoying life at school and learning at the same time. All I truly hoped for at my young age. They had party times at the dorm, and it was exciting to be living in the down town area—lots of nice restaurants—fun disco spots—movie theatres, and I was able to participate in all of the things. On top of it all, I was doing well in school.

Laurie indeed blossomed at school and Bill and I were thrilled that it was working for her and glad that we had found such a good solution to help her back on her feet. Finally something was going well for her—she deserved the good times.

All too soon, it was graduation time. Naturally I was happy to have completed everything, and I had done well in all of the courses, but it meant the end to some fun friendships, and moving on into the business world.

Finding a job in the travel industry is not always the easiest thing if you are looking strictly at travel agencies—Laurie however found a niche in a Car Rental Company. One that had it's national headquarters in a near town, and that's where she worked, and enjoyed it very much.

I was pleased to be working for the car rental company. I especially liked working at the International Desk and was dealing with far away countries. I again found it to be a learning situation, but this time making money rather than paying money for the education. I worked with a friendly group of people and was finding great calm and contentment in my life which I hadn't felt for a long time. I now had hopes of a future that I hadn't thought about in quite some time—friends, both female and male, and going out for good times with them was most enjoyable.

Of course there was stress with the job—I doubt if there are many jobs where one doesn't encounter that, but it began to take a toll on me.

Laurie started developing some health problems. It made us feel apprehensive, but this time we were sure that if we got a handle on things right away we could get things resolved. It proved a little more difficult than we had anticipated.

Chapter 9
Checking Danger Signals

So many things were finally working out, but Laurie started to have stomach pains, similar to ones she had suffered with at the time of her break down, so she went back to see her original psychiatrist who of course said everything was just fine, but he did prescribe some Pamelar for her, but that made her extremely tired and she was finding it almost impossible to carry on with her job as she would literally fall asleep at her desk, and her attendance record suffered She then went through various tests both with her GP doctor and a Gynecologist to rule out any physical possibilities for the pains.

Finally they concluded that all tests were fine, and the pains were indeed psychological. Bill and I knew how to deal with that, but Laurie didn't, and every day grew harder for her, and we were becoming fearful that if she didn't receive help, she may fall back into some possible mental problems.

I didn't know exactly how to deal with my pain. I was told it was all in my head. That frightened me. I had gone through enough dealing with "imaginary" situations a few years back. Of course I still held fears that possibly I may have a set back. I'm sure that my folks still feared that also. All I really knew was that I actually felt pain and I was hurting.

In desperation I once again called her first primary Psychiatrist and asked if she could be hospitalized for a few days just to help her get through this period. He said he certainly couldn't do that. I asked if we could take her in ourselves, but he said no we couldn't do that either. Next I asked if her medical doctor could have her hospitalized, but he said that wouldn't be possible. He finally simply said "I'll have to hang up on you now, Mrs. Campbell."

I pleaded and begged reminding him that 3 years earlier no one would help us and we had to go through a messy scene where police had to be called and we didn't want a repeat of that. Finally I asked if he would at least talk to her, but he said that he was booked up for quite a while. At that point I said "Thanks a lot for nothing", and that was the end of the conversation.

I don't give up easily, and I called another clinic—pleaded and did get an immediate appointment with a Psychiatrist there.

When we arrived, he asked me in for about 15 minutes and talked to Laurie and I together to verify some information. Finally someone who acknowledged that I may actually have a relationship with her. In one appointment he was able to recognize that Laurie was dealing with extreme nervous tension and prescribed a tranquillizer to calm her.

That got her through a tough time, and I was indeed thankful. She then began to relax and the pains subsided. After not too long a period of time, she was able to stop using the tranquillizers and finally all was going well, and she was once again heading back to "normal".

I was grateful that someone listened to me and helped me talk through some of my fears. He assured me that it was just a matter of dealing with some of the stresses that I was under, and gave me a prescription for some tranquillizers. Perhaps part of it was having someone tell me that it was a "normal" reaction and didn't just tell me it was all in my head.

Bill and I were so thankful that we were able to find someone to help her—we were again feeling frustrations and not knowing where to go next. She had been doing so well that it caught us off guard when she seemed to be hurting so and worried that it would be a set back both in her job and for herself.

Laurie and I had discussed her fears of having another break down and how she would know what to do. I assured her that if she ever started having strange feelings such as had happened before, she would recognize them. The difference being that she would know to seek out help right away before slipping into the depths of fear and lose reality.

This short "relapse" seemed to reassure her that she needn't be so fearful. Of course it made Bill and I more sure that she would be able to do just fine taking care of herself and that she knew enough to seek help if and when she needed it.

Chapter 10
Correspondence

In 1990, Laurie was very impressed by an article she read in the Minneapolis Star Tribune in July. There still wasn't too much ever being written about Mental Health Issues, unless it was an unfortunate incident that involved a crime or some terrible accident.

I felt that it was an excellent letter, so we decided to print excerpts of it as an ending of this book to show you how candid she could now be and how the healing had indeed taken place.

Here is an excerpt of the article which she had read.

"Have a look in your own mirror for a glimpse of mental illness"
By Mark S. Goulston. LA Times

Why do we ignore the mentally ill and their presence? If our avoidance isn't willful, how can we explain society's continued neglect of them? Funding is consistently curtailed for mental health centers, but needs increase. Lack of funding forces professionals to turn away persons in dire need, and even bed others down on pallets on the floor.

Prisoners are guaranteed a bed. There are no guarantees for the fragile mentally ill who need help. So often we fear them. The truth is that we all have suffered from moments of temporary insanity. When we are driving and see a policeman we slow down,—temporary paranoia. We may take an idea and add meanings, altering its importance out of context with reality—perhaps that's temporary psychosis.

When we feel we can do anything without regard to consequences, we suffer temporary mania. When we feel so down we can't do anything, we have temporary depression. When we try to get ahead at someone else's expense—temporary sociopath.

Often, the mentally ill are still treated as though the illness is a moral failing—that they could be well if they just "cleaned up their act." giving the mentally ill no support, and feeling alone.

If any of us were frozen in one of our temporary moments of insanity and stigmatized like the mentally ill, what would we see on faces of those around us?

Even the faces of ones you love the most could show fear, disdain, pity and even avoidance.

When we admit our vulnerabilities and fears that bind us with the mentally ill, perhaps we can confront and conquer ourselves. Now Laurie's letter:

July 18, 1990

I am writing in reply to an article submitted by Professor Mark Goulston that was published in the Minneapolis Tribune Sunday Editorial (See copy attached).

Professor Goulston: thank you for reminding us of the vulnerability of the human psyche, and the fact that none of us are immune to the possibility of mental illness.

Society needs to be reminded of this fact; for the stigma that is attached to those considered mentally ill is far too damaging. The mentally ill have been shunned by society. Coming out of the dark ages took too long, and the inhuman treatments scarred too many. We must hope that society continues to make the step ahead. We cannot just leave the advances that have only come about so recently.

I remember reading a biography of a beautiful movie star, Francis Farmer. I was in high school at the time and still recall the impact the novel left with me. This movie star had suddenly attained stardom in her early twenties, and had everything going for her. Just as suddenly, she was hit with mental illness.

Her stardom ruined! Even with money available to help, she still continued to be plagued with depressions and breakdowns. Even with the help and support of those who continued to support and love her, she was never able to live a full and happy life. It was so sad—she attained a dream that so many wish for, yet for her, fate dealt her unhappiness and confusion Could her destiny have been changed? Could it have been changed today? Good questions. At that time I thought that mental illness must be the worst sickness that could happen to anyone. I thought to myself that I could handle any physical handicap better than mental illness. I was seventeen then. There was no mental illness in my family history or at least none that myself or my family were aware of.

A year later, I was attending the University of Wisconsin in River Falls. Two months before Christmas break I started thinking new thoughts. Profound ideas came to me. I felt powerful. Everything was great.

At this point she went on to describe to him many of the same facts and happenings as we have written about in this book.

I was now becoming scared. My friends would say something to me, and I couldn't remember their questions or conversations because so many thoughts were shooting through my mind. I couldn't concentrate on what was being said.

I didn't want to tell anyone what was happening to me because I was sure they would throw me in some mental ward, tie me up and lock me in a padded cell. This was in 1975, and I wasn't that far off from the fact that it well could have happened that way.

Unfortunately, in places this still really did happen—the fears, diagnosis that weren't made, lack of treatments—a part of the medical system that few wanted to delve into. Sad to report that even now, there are many reports of mistreatment that still happen—affecting numerous lives.

I was sure the whole world was in hell. I figured we were all in this together. I didn't want to be in hell, and somehow I would pull myself and everyone else through this whole ordeal. I still had faith that God would pull me through, even if everyone else had given up. Pity those who have no faith.

My mother should write a book from her point of view and the feelings of helplessness they went through because they couldn't legally get help for me. I was 18, I had to ask for help, and I did not know how to. How unfair! Anyway, I finally was admitted to the hospital after attacking my mother. It's a scary thought; could I have possibly killed her? Hopefully the fact that deep down I knew that she was my mother, and that I am really a loving and caring person, made me incapable of doing my mother any deep harm. A nightmare in real life that we both lived through. If only help lines, etc would have been available at that time.

True that by this time there were some help lines available, but not always handled in ways that gave real direction to people in a confused state, but at least it was finally acknowledged that indeed this is a real health problem.

That was my first experience with the scope of the human mind, and also my first experience with other people's concept of mental illness. I could only remember what my personality had been like before the breakdown, and that became my challenge—to once again become the person that I knew I had been.

You have read all of the trials that she and indeed all of us lived through while she fought to attain her goals and challenges, and indeed she did.

This letter unfolded as I began to write. I can only end by saying how thankful I am that you, Professor Goulston, and others like you continue to work in determining the causes and effects of mental health—whether or not it stems from genetics, chemical imbalances or societies pressures. Thank you for continuing the work of enlightening public awareness and taking the whole broad spectrum out of the dark ages.

Thankfully yours,

Laurie Campbell

She did receive a reply from him. (see below).

Dear Ms. Campbell,

Thank you for the copy of your letter to the editor of the Mpls. Star Tribune.

You write clearly and well of your situation. You have courage and perseverance and should be proud of yourself.

Enclosed find another piece you might like.

Best Regards,
Mark S. Goulston, M.D.

Here are excerpts of the enclosed piece that he sent.

"Stigma—Our Secret Social Virus"
By Mark S. Goulston, LA Times

The American Psychiatric Assn. Met in San Francisco in May of 1989, and discussed Overcoming Stigma. However, every day hundreds of people will be stigmatized, possibly for life. The following examples trigger in us a reaction of avoidance:

A suicide attempt, AIDS diagnosis, rape or child abuse, racial or religious harassment, physical or mental disabilities, homelessness or revelation of "skeletons in the closet" of a prominent person. When these people are identified, they are pushed away and they feel isolated. Because of a difference that is out of their control, they are categorized and pushed away.

Stigma keeps them distant—less contagious to the rest of us. Stigma allows us to put them in categories so we don't have to think about them. What should we do?

We keep a steadfast refusal to see their fear and hurt and will do anything to keep from being pulled into their world. Perhaps we are afraid, seeing our own vulnerability.

If we can maintain our view of these people as different, perhaps we reassure ourselves that their traumas and tragedies will never happen to us.

Stigma can be reduced by empathy and compassion and they cannot be rushed. You can't identify with and alienate at the same moment. There is a neurotic dilemma in many of us. We feel entitled to a good life, but perhaps feel we don't deserve it because to get what we want, we cut corners. We may take advantage of people in order to get our way, but we know we have done something wrong and we feel ashamed.

When we give to others and give more than we take and don't shortchange the world, it is then that we earn, gain and deserve happiness and peace of mind. These will be our big payoffs.

July 28, 1990

Professor Goulston,

I thank you for reading my letter and for sending a reply. I had a difficult time tracking you down. I'm glad to find that you are alive and well and still working and writing. You are very sympathetic and I can sense the discouragement you have come across for others.

I am doing fine now, but it was a long time before I really felt like a whole person again. I've learned a great deal about emotions and the thinking process. I've been fortunate to have made new relationships with wonderful persons, and also fortunate for having good strong family ties.

As I at first struggled back from my break down, I felt worthless and uninteresting. I had a difficult time accepting myself, but human nature as it is, we continue to seek our friends—eventually people continued to seek me out, and I could let them be a part of my life.

I am fortunate that this incident occurred when I was young. I was able to overcome obstacles on my own. How much more would have been at stake if it had happened now, when it also would have meant coming back to my job and regaining my responsibilities. Who would take care of me now?

The stigma I felt at 18 was so strong that I could tell no one about the incident. I had to understand it myself. It took many years of self counseling, analyzing and questioning to come to grips with my ego and let go of the stigma I had attached to mental illness. The skeletons in the closet will never hurt me—they've turned to dust.

I was always amazed by how accepting people were of me though. Because of good people in my life and proper channels others gave to me when I was in need, I found they listened to me and many times put themselves out for me.

Because of what happened to me, Professor, I think that I have been given the grace to be free from any stigma. God willing, may I be able to carry that feeling throughout my life. I want to GIVE more than I TAKE from this world.

Thank you for your continued work, understanding and writing. Perhaps some day I'll be of help to someone because of my experiences. Hopefully, perhaps I already have, as I have tried to in any situation when I felt it would be of some use.

Best wishes to you and your continued endeavors—
Laurie Campbell

Chapter 11
Confidence Regained by Everyone

As the weeks grew into months and things seemed to remain on an even keel, we all found a new peace in our every day living. Our home life was back to the comfortable relaxed setting that we always had taken for granted, until it was so terribly shaken by all of the stressful disruptions.

Luckily, our young son seemed to have come through all of the events with no visible emotional affects. His relationship and love for Laurie had never seemed to shatter, and we were thankful for that. We had finally found the help that we needed—gotten through this fearful set back in our lives, but finding satisfaction in knowing that it did not damage the love we all have for one another. It only made it stronger. Our faith in God and one another grew also.

My husband could once again direct his energy into his work without dark shadows of worry following him.

Laurie was doing well at work, received raises and promotions—indeed it was a calmness fully appreciated.

As I was able to finally feel good, I was able to do better at work and find happiness being with people and doing fun things. I began to worry less and less about the "what ifs" about situations. I just found that I was able to handle things pretty well by myself, and didn't always have to analyze every situation. I could be spontaneous and feel that people were having a good time when we were together, not looking at me to watch my reactions or give me a strange look if I happened to say something that didn't necessarily seem appropriate to them. I was truly once again enjoying myself.

Laurie was living in an apartment now, and I knew that she could handle it. There were a few times when she would call and, as I mentioned once before, I'd hear her voice and know that she was feeling down. I guess by this time I had become a fill in psychologist, as I knew that she just needed to be talked to, and as the conversation went on, I would bring it up a level into a happier zone, and soon the voice would start to have a smile in it, and eventually we'd share some laughs. She was really a delight, and I loved to talk to her. My only concern was in wondering how things would go if anything happened to Bill and I. Who would she be able to call then? Would she revert back to a depression and hide in the darkness? This was my fear that I couldn't quite shake for a while.

I was enjoying having my own place to take care of, and being able to do what I wanted to do when I wanted to do it. On the whole, all was going well. There were a few times, I suppose when things didn't go right at work or when I'd have an argument with my boy friend that I'd get down. However, by now I knew that everyone has times when they are down about things and I didn't stand alone in that aspect. Mostly it was because I still had self doubts about myself being able to handle bad or sad times. It was at times like that when I really wanted to talk to Mom. She is such an optimistic person, and I wanted it to rub off on me. Somehow, magically when I would talk to her, some of that happiness would just travel along the phone lines. She had a way of turning the conversation around to something else, and I'd get through the bad spots.

I finally felt that those times were getting less and less. Soon I could divert my feelings and I guess I had just learned how to look at the silver linings and count my blessings, which were, of course, many.

Laurie's dealings with unhappy situations began to improve. She didn't have nearly as many times when she would sound "down" on the telephone conversations. Now there were a lot more times when the conversations were simply sharing. She telling me things that happened—what had transpired, and how it had been resolved. Thus my fears of her relying on us became less and less. She had matured and grown so emotionally that I became most confident that she knew how to handle herself and other people. She was no longer dependent on me as backup. She was completely in control. What a great feeling.

Mom was always there for me when I needed her, but as time went on, I realized that I could take on more without getting boggled—fearing that I wouldn't be able to handle it. I built up my emotional strength—actually surprising myself, but I could do it with fewer struggles as time passed, and not be worrying over things.

Finally everyone in the family knew that she'd do just fine. Perhaps the real test was the fact that she was married. I wasn't fully sure of her choice, but if she was happy, then I'd be happy for her. For a few years, things were OK, but then things began to fall apart. I knew this, but I didn't want to interfere and kept myself from saying anything—until she finally talked to me.

My marriage was not going well. My husband was proving more and more to me that I had made a poor choice. Soon I was extremely unhappy and not liking the feeling at all. I knew that he was unhappy also. It was going from bad to worse, and his verbal abuse of me was getting nasty. Our arguments became a practically ongoing situation and not doing any good for either of us. We began to talk about divorce. I felt that we should be trying more, but counseling did not help. Eventually we were divorced, but life went on. I found I could handle it and get on with life by myself.

I was actually not worried about Laurie's mental state at all when she was divorced. In fact I was impressed as to how she became able to pick up her life and handle everything by herself. She continued living in her home on acreage. Continuing not just taking care of her horses, but boarding other horses to bring in some extra income. She was of course holding down a regular job, so it was no small task, but she did it. We were so proud of her, and we knew that she would also be able to handle whatever situations may arrive in her future.

Going through the divorce and being on my own again actually seemed to build up my strength. I knew what I wanted out of life and knew it was up to me to achieve new goals. Sure it was tough at times, and my Dad came over and helped me with some physical chores where four strong hands were needed. Thankfully he was always willing to be there, and we had fun working together. I seemed to be able to go forward, and was able financially to pretty well stay on top of things.

I finally had full confidence that I could work for the things I wanted and was in full control of my future, and willing to work hard to achieve my dreams. Thankfully I still have dreams and goals, but for now, thanks to the love of my folks and my family, I'm living a good life. God has showered me with many blessings.

Laurie has moved on and continued to better her life. She now is a proud owner of a home surrounded by several acres, has her horses, dogs and cats and is living in an environment that she enjoys. We are always happy to have her company as she is truly a delight to be with. She is admired by many, and we consistently have people tell us how much they enjoy her. We couldn't be prouder, but we know a little more about her achievements than others, as we know the struggles that she had as a teenager. Because of it possibly, she has a beauty and strength that most people may only hope at some point in their lives to attain.

She shares all of this with many people and enriches the lives of everyone she touches.

Chapter 12
Types of Mental Illnesses and Treatments

Mental Illness has been around since time began. (MHA)

Descriptions of "Demon possessed" people are described in the Bible. Think of how many "witches" were burned at the stake—again thinking of them as possessed. Many of these poor souls were undoubtedly victims displaying forms of mental illnesses. No one knew what to do with these people—with heartbreak, many of them had to place them in "insane asylums"—hoping that it would at least be a place to harbor them and feed them and hopefully see that they would not be harmed—that's all that could be expected. Many who were kept at home were hidden in closets or in locked rooms, perhaps even chained to a bed or to a wall so no one would find out about them, but all lived with the heartbreak of not being able to help them.

Very little was being done to really discover what was going on in the minds of these people, thereby possibly finding some help for them.

Dr. Walter Freeman—

According to a Public Television Documentary aired in January of 2008, In 1936, some research was done that led to the discovery that something in the frontal lobes of people seemed to have some effect on their behavior. Through this discovery, Dr. Walter Freeman started the drastic treatments of Lobotomies. It was indeed rather barbaric, but for many it was a way to perhaps free men and women.

No one stood in his way to try this surgical method of cutting nerves to the frontal lobes. At first he drilled holes in the skull to perform this. There was success in this first type of operation, but after months, many developed other, even worse problems.

Then he came up with a method—using an "ice pick" type of instrument which he pounded in through a person's eye ball. This method took only 5 minutes, and was done in an office. Now however, other medical persons were watching and feeling that this was not always a cure, and, in fact was sometimes disastrous.

He began going to Mental Institutions—hoping to free people from these places and give them and their families peace and joy. Many were indeed calmed enough to be able to go back to their homes—the majority of them not exactly like they had been when younger, but at least able to live without violence and being feared. He would perform these like an assembly line—doing 25-75 of them a day. In 1949, 5,000 were treated using this method. Although it didn't bring many back to "normal", it gave people hope that their loved ones could possibly be helped.

Of course not all who had Lobotomies were helped—some went on to become vegetables, and to some it proved fatal. In the mid 50's, others in the medical field realized that destroying part of the brain was not a cure by any means. Then came a discovery that drugs could make a difference. In the 1950's, **Thorazine** was found to bring relief.

In 1960, Dr. Freeman moved to California, and started giving lobotomies to "unruly" children (nineteen of them under age eighteen—one even four years old.) By 1968, Dr. Freeman had performed 29,000 lobotomies, and was finally stripped of his medical credentials when the last patient died of a brain hemorrhage. (PBS 2008)

Perhaps he was totally convinced that he had brought about a "miracle" to release suffering souls. What a sad ending for someone who at least was trying to help creatures afflicted with Mental Illnesses and though he may be criticized, he at least opened up a new field for others to research and hopefully help these "lost souls". He died in 1972.

THORAZINE

Ironically, according to Say NO to Psychiatry and featured by FTR— the Foundation for Truth in Reality, states as follows:

Thorazine has been called a "chemical lobotomy" because of the similar effects it creates. Briefly, a lobotomy destroys partially or completely all functioning of the frontal lobes. The frontal lobes are unique to human beings and are the seat of the higher functions such as love, concern for others, empathy, self-insight, creativity, initiative, autonomy, rationality, abstract reasoning, judgment, future planning, foresight, willpower, determination and concentration. Without the frontal lobes it is impossible to be "human" in the fullest sense of the word' they are required for a civilized, effective, mature life. Without this "human" aspect a person is incapable of living a rewarding, happy and responsible life.

To fully understand the nature and effects of drugs such as Thorazine it is useful to go back and see what the early research psychiatrists themselves had to say about the drug. The two pioneers of Thorazine, Delay and Deniker, said about small doses of the drug in 1952:

"Sitting or lying, the patient is motionless in his bed, often pale And with eyelids lowered. He remains silent most of the time. If he is questioned, he answers slowly and deliberately in a Monotonous and indifferent voice; he expresses himself in a Few words and becomes silent:.

In 1954 Thorazine began flooding the state mental hospitals. The narcoleptics are synonymous with tranquilizers and anti psychotics. This excerpt from the Boston Globe in 1988, states

The narcoleptics are the drug most commonly given to schizophrenics. Drugs such as Thorazine were touted to "cure" the patient by repairing or altering "bad" brain chemistry (whatever that means...).

But the truth is the drug involves a strong dulling of the mind and emotional functions, and that this is what acts to inhibit or

:push the symptoms into the back ground:,. According to Jerry Avon, M.D,.:

My concern is that people are having their minds blunted in a way that probably does diminish their capacity to appreciate life:.(Breggin)

Like surgical lobotomy, chemical lobotomy has no specific beneficial effect on any human problem or human being. It puts a chemical clamp on the higher brain of anyone.

In Tranquilizing of America (1979), Richard Hughes and Robert Brewin state:

"When used on a large population of institutionalized persons, as they are, they can help keep the house in order with the minimum program of activities and rehabilitation and the minimum number of attendants, aides, nurses, and doctors".

No hiding the obvious real purpose of the drug. It saves money for the institutions and makes the people more manageable. Neuroleptic use is not rare or unusual. In fact,

"On many psychiatric wards the narcoleptics are given to 90 to 100 percent of the patients; in many nursing home, to 50% or more of the old people; and in many institutions for persons with mental retardation, to 50% or more of the inmates. Neuroleptics are also used in children's facilities and in prisons." (Peter Breggin, Toxic Psychiatry.)

Neuroleptics are also used in tranquilizing darts for subduing wild animals and in injections to permit the handling of domestic animals who become vicious. The veterinary use of narcoleptics so undermines their anti psychotic theory that young psychiatrists are not taught about it.

"The brain-disabling principle applies to all of the most potent Psychiatric interventions—narcoleptics, antidepressants, lithium, electroshock, and psychosurgery. None of these correct or improve existing brain dysfunction, such as any presumed biochemical Imbalance. If the patient happens to suffer from brain dysfunction, then the psychiatric drug, electroshock, or psychosurgery will worsen or compound it.

In summary, Thorazine and all narcoleptics, cause chemical lobotomies with no specific therapeutic effect on any symptoms or problems. Their main impact is to blunt and subdue the individual. They also physically paralyze the body, acting as a chemical straightjacket. Additionally, these drugs are the cause of a plague of brain damage effecting up to half or more of long-term patients. Much of this information came from Peter Breggin's book Toxic Psychiatry.

(Breggin)

SCHIZOPHRENIA

Symptoms of schizophrenia
Hearing voices not heard by others
Believing that others are reading their minds,
Controlling their thoughts or conspiring
Against them
Hallucinations or delusions

Schizophrenia also affects the behavior of those suffering

Typical are:
Aloofness or being withdrawn
Appearing detached or preoccupied with things
That may not be real.
Being immobile for hours, uttering sounds,
Being completely rigid
Relentless urge to move or having to do things and
Not being able to sit still
Being wide-awake, extremely vigilant and alert.
Schizophrenia patients are often extremely agitated.

These unusual behaviors can make other people feel uncomfortable and sometimes even scare them.

Psychotic episodes

During a psychotic episode, people with schizophrenia cannot think logically and may lose all sense of who they are and who others are. Everyday tasks such as: thinking clearly, controlling emotions, making decisions and relating to others become difficult. The severity of the symptoms and the long-lasting, chronic pattern of the illness often result in severe disability. Treatment involves taking the appropriate medication and getting personal support.

Medication

This is a necessary part of the treatment. The challenge is to find the medication which helps you in the best possible way, with the least side-effects possible. It is of the utmost importance to initiate treatment as soon as possible—in which case you have a higher chance that you will be able to lead a normal life and that problems don't get worse.

Often times, patients do not take their medication as they should, for various reasons, some being:

No immediate noticeable effect of the treatment
Incomplete response
Side-effects
Starting to feel better
Lack of responsibility
Forgetfulness
Running out of medication
Denying being in a condition that needs treatment.

Psychosocial Treatment

Medication alone is not a complete treatment, so combining it with Psychosocial treatments is recommended.

Aspects of this treatment include:

Rehabilitation,
Individual psychotherapy
Family intervention.

Family, friends, and peer groups can provide support and encourage a person with schizophrenia in readjusting to normal life. Set goals must be achievable, as pressuring or criticizing will probably cause the patient to experience stress. This will result in a worsening of symptoms. Like anyone else, people with schizophrenia need to know when they are doing things right. A positive approach will be helpful and more effective than criticism.

(Q & A: What is Bipolar Disorder?)

DEPRESSION

There are many faces of Mental Illness—Depression is one that is wide spread. The US Surgeon General estimates depression affects at least 20 million people a year. (Inserted)

The World Health Organisation (WHO) estimates that each year approximately one million people die from suicide, which represents a global mortality rate of 16 people per 100,000 or one death every 40 seconds. It is predicted that by 2020 the rate of death will increase to one every 20 seconds.

The WHO further reports that:

- In the last 45 years suicide rates have increased by 60% worldwide. Suicide is now among the three leading causes of death among those aged 15-44 (male and female). Suicide attempts are up to 20 times more frequent than completed suicides.
- Although suicide rates have traditionally been highest amongst elderly males, rates among young people have been

increasing to such an extent that they are now the group at highest risk in a third of all countries.

• Mental health disorders (particularly depression and substance abuse) are associated with more than 90% of all cases of suicide.

• However, suicide results from many complex sociocultural factors and is more likely to occur during periods of socioeconomic, family and individual crisis (e.g. loss of a loved one, unemployment, sexual orientation, difficulties with developing one's identity, disassociation from one's community or other social/belief group, and honour). http://www.befrienders.org/info/index.asp?PageURL=statistics.php

As seems to be true of many forms of mental illness, the victim seems to be able to hide it from people who don't know them well, and won't accept help from people who do know them well. Unfortunately, many only see one cure for their malady.

Depression can hide other health problems. These can remain unnoticed and untreated in people with depression. In some cases, physical symptoms such as headaches, stomach pain or nausea, constant back or neck aches, and even breathing problems.

Depression is the number one cause of suicides. (webmed)

In 2002, former WCCO-TV (Minneapolis, MN) news anchor Randi Kay's father took his own life. He died from a disease she never knew he had—depression. She shared her story in the May 2003 issue of Minnesota Monthly magazine.

Perhaps people in such a confused state feel that there is no hope, and it would be easier on the loved ones they leave behind—not thinking of the devastation they will feel.

As Randi states, "My father's depression and suicide has changed me. Losing a loved one to suicide is torture. There are so many unknowns, what ifs, and why nots. Often, suicide survivors express a desire to die too. For some months, I felt like death was perched on my shoulder, that I was next. My father's death has changed me forever. Not a day goes by that I don't think of him in his final moment. Did he cry? Was he calm? Did he think of me? Didn't he know how much we still needed him? Was he angry? Why did he have to hurry death?"

At least 70 percent of all suicides are caused by untreated depression. Across the country, 500,000 people kill themselves each year. In Minnesota, 500

Depression does not suddenly show up like a case of measles and fade as quickly as a rash—it develops slowly, working from the inside out. By the time it becomes evident to other people, the disease has caused inner erosion and scars that some find just too difficult to overcome.

There are at least hot lines to call this day of age, but too often the person going through depression does not call out themselves. If you are suspicious that one of your loved ones may be going through some trauma, please reach out for help.

The San Francisco Suicide Prevention and Befrienders International have listed some Warning Signs of Suicide. (Befrienders)

Remarks such as "I can't go on" or
"Everybody will be better off without me."
Depression or withdrawal
Reckless behavior
Giving away possessions
Drug or alcohol abuse
Major loss or life change.
Change in behavior, personality, or appearance
Diminished sexual interest
Sudden loss of appetite or overeating
Low self-esteem
Lack of hope for future.

Treatments for depression include Psychotherapy, and Antidepressant drugs, which can improve mood, sleep, appetite, and concentration. However, it can take from 6 to 12 weeks before real signs of improvement are experienced for some medications.

On the whole, a combination of the two types of treatment seems to be the most effective way of treating depression.

Living with someone suffering from depression can be very stressful for families—support of loved ones is most necessary.

Bipolar Disorders
(Formerly called manic depression)

Bipolar disorder, is one of the most common mental disorders. Typical for Bipolar disorders are unusual swings in a person's mood, energy level and ability to function. People suffering from it experience difficulties in keeping a job, or finishing school. They often suffer from damaged relationships. Often it is not recognized as an illness, and people sometimes suffer for years before being diagnosed and receiving proper therapy. (What Is Bipolar Disorder?)

These patients experience dramatic mood swings, ranging from being extremely 'high' to feeling very depressed, sad and hopeless. Then often back again to the 'high' stage. These periods of highs and lows are called episodes of mania and depression (My Optum Health.)

Psychosis can be a symptom of bipolar disorder.

Severe episodes of mania or depression can include the symptoms of psychosis. They may have hallucinations: they may hear, see or sense the presence of certain things that are not actually there.

Another symptom is delusions: patients have false but strong beliefs that can not logically be explained. (webmed)

The type of psychotic symptoms reflects the mood of the patients. during a manic episode, they may believe to be a person with special powers or wealth. During depressive episodes, they can believe to be worthless, or to be ruined or to be guilty of some crime. (Mental Health: Types of Mental Illness)

Bipolar disorder: mixed bipolar state

Sometimes the symptoms of depression and mania may happen together.

Patients often are agitated, have troubles sleeping, sometimes even suffer psychosis or have suicidal thoughts. They may on one hand feel sad, but at the same time feeling very energetic.

Clinical implications

There are now effective treatment methods that make it possible for people with bipolar disorder to lead a full and productive life. Important is not to wait too long before therapy is started. If therapy starts early, there is better chance that the cumbersome manic and depressive episodes can be reduced.

Medications prescribed for this disorder—

Anti psychotics—of particular value for the treatment of acute mania and relieving psychotic symptoms

Lithium—long given as a first-time treatment to control mania and to prevent recurrences of both manic and depressive periods

Anticonvulsants—they work as a mood stabilizer—sometimes in combination with lithium

Benzodiazepines—May be valuable to promote better sleep in patients suffering from insomnia—however, can become habit forming

Bipolar disorder recurs across the life span of the patients. However, most patients are free of symptoms between episodes.

Bipolar I disorder More "classical" form, where patients have recurrent episodes of mania and depression.

Bipolar II People do not develop severe mania, but rather experience milder episodes of hypomania which alternate with depression.

Long term outcome of bipolar disorder with proper treatment.

When treated adequately, people with bipolar can lead a healthy and productive life. Mostly, therapy will help reduce the frequency and the severity of both the depressive and manic episodes, so the patients can enjoy a good quality of life. (My Optum Health)

As much as we would hope that things would look promising in the future for the diagnosis and treatment of Mental Illness, perhaps we find ourselves striving more to diagnose what "NORMAL" is.

People with mental illness often have problems getting treatment.

There are two reasons for this. One is finding the right kind of services available, but not every service is available in every county.

The other problem involves funding. Treatment is paid for either through a public system or a private insurance system.

The cost of mental illness to the individual, the family and society is enormous. Mental illness often prevents a person from being productive at work—or even being able to go to work. Half of all visits to doctors are related to mental illness issues.

People with mental illness fill more hospital beds than those with cancer, lung and heart disease combined. Suicide is three times more common than murder.

Wisconsin law requires health insurers to provide at least $7,000 per year of coverage. In many cases, that is all private insurance will provide. And insurance companies have the right to refuse to offer a policy to a person with mental illness (or any other "pre-existing" condition. Mental illness services can be costly. Weekly visits with a mental health professional could use up that amount before years end. Inpatient treatment costs over $1,500/ day in Wisconsin. To pay for these services out of pocket is often not possible, so people go without. Help.

There are more and more statistics gathered telling of the problems finding help, and the difficulties in getting and paying for treatments, but no real solutions seem to be found.

As found in the book "Bipolar Disorder Demystified, by Lana R. Castle,—published in 2003, we read:

A young friend recently sought her first psychiatrist consult for Depression. Getting in for her first visit took three months. Because her insurance plan doles out only one referral at a time, if the first doctor didn't work out and she needed a second referral, she'd have to face another long wait. Three or more months is a long time to go without treatment, particularly if a depression worsens.

A Shortage of Community-Based Services.

For those who even seek treatment—now estimated at one third of those who truly need it—waiting lists are long, appointments scheduled much too far apart, and quality time with trained professionals tightly controlled. People enter the hospital when things get desperate, then often wind up on the streets within a few days.

That's one reason so many homeless people display mental illness.

Lack of Treatment or Under-treatment

Stigma prevents many seriously ill people from even seeking help. By the time we begin treatment—often in the midst of a major episode—scrambled neural pathways may be so well established that our brains are much harder to stabilize. Disordered thinking may be so deeply ingrained that it takes years to turn it around. Government programs such as Supplemental Security Income and Social Security Disability Insurance—both administered by the Social Security Administration—do provide a modest income for Individuals with severe mental illness. But funds are limited, Initial applications are denied half of the time, and appeals often take a year or more.

Due partially to the lack of community-based services, increasing numbers of people with mental illness wind up in jail. This is particularly true of those who lack insurance, jobs, and homes.

Experts estimate that up to 20% of incarcerated individuals have a severe mental illness. (Castle)

In all of the reading and research that I have come upon, everything seems to be telling people who are going through all of this what they can do—assuming that they are all adults who are in a position to make decisions about and take care of themselves.

I have as yet not found out much about how persons, like Laurie was, "adult" according to law, but not holding jobs and not having their own insurance, etc. are supposed to find help. I'm sure she is not the only one in that age category to have to find solutions. Obviously there may be many simply slipping through the cracks, perhaps never finding help. Such scary thoughts.

Indeed this whole issue of mental illness seems to be reaching the Dreaded Pandemic proportions in the medical field, without a Magic "cure all" vaccine available to stop it's spread.

The medical profession seems to be working diligently in research to find treatments and cures for AIDS, Cancer, Heart Disease, and so many more diseases, yet Mental Illness statistics just seem to continue growing, and affecting a wider age span than any of the above. A most frightening future in so many ways.

Thankfully, since the 1970's, with increased awareness, there is hope.

Still, further research must go on, and hopefully medical fields will find new treatments that will benefit the many who are in need.

Chapter 13
Ongoing Episodes—Do the Stigmas Remain?

Excerpts from newspaper articles printed between the years 2000 to 2009

"Mental Illness Is No Laughing Matter"
By Sharon Autio—July, 2000

The majority of the time, the entertainment media portrays persons suffering from mental illnesses not only in negative, but false stereotypes. Often they are depicted as murderers, vicious attackers—evil bad doers. A shameful stereotype.

If not in that aspect, often they are shown as acting in nonsensical foolish ways, giving audiences just a good laugh. But at who's expense? It misinforms and perpetuates the stigma that may discourage people with mental problems from seeking treatment.

Persons with "split personalities" are called schizophrenic, when indeed it is now known as dissociative identity disorder, and is very rare. Most people with schizophrenia are not violent and they do indeed not pose a danger to anyone. More often, they are victims of violence rather than causing it.

Granted distortions in the field of entertainment are common, and in many cases harmless. What is disturbing is that Mental Illness is perhaps one of the last stigmas of the 20th century and one that affects many people who in real life are not violent and, with treatment get better, work, play and have family and friends.

The field of entertainment doesn't take on AIDS, cancer or other tragic diseases. The reason is that none of them, including Mental illness are just not funny

"New Tool in Treating Mental Disorders"
By Judy Foreman

Brain scanning may be close to revolutionizing psychiatry, a field in medicine where doctor's guesses are still the most common way to figure out what's wrong.

It's still not used for routine diagnosis for mental ills, but can be used in understanding abnormalities including obsessive compulsive disorder, schizophrenia, anxiety and depression.

At UCLA, doctors are experimenting with PET scans to find which patients will respond to the antidepressant drug Paxil.

The lead researcher, Dr. Sanjayua Saxena, associate director of the UCLA Obsessive Compulsive Disorder Research Program have potential to identify brain patterns that predict a response to therapy for both OCD and depression.

At Massachusetts General Hospital, Dr. Scott Rauch has long been using PET and other scans in psychiatric care. Rauch and his colleagues have used scans to predict how well people with OCD respond to surgery in which doctors interrupt pathways through tiny cuts. They are now trying implanting permanent electrodes into the affected tissue, called deep-brain stimulation, already used to treat Parkinson's disease.

Elsewhere, researchers are using other types of scans to probe other psychiatric afflictions.MRIs are used to study Attention Deficit Hyperactivity Disorder in children.

Other researchers are using functional MRI (fMRI) to study abnormalities in schizophrenia and other disorders.

Brain scans may never substitute for intuitive guesswork, but they will be useful in helping doctors figure out which patients are most likely to respond to treatments.

"More being treated for depression, but poorly, study says"

Treatment rats for major depression have improved, but more than half of patients are getting inadequate therapy, a new study suggests.

While the stigma of mental illness may be lessening, many doctors may not be aware of advancements in help. Also, many patients may be seeking unproven therapies, according to Harvard Medical School researcher Ronald Kessler.

In studies of 9,090 adults ages 18 and up, it was found that 57% with recent major depression had received treatment. Nearly 40% high than in the 1980s.

Only in 21% of patients were treatments considered adequate or adhering to accepted guidelines. This was based on findings published in the journal of American Medical Association based on evaluations from February 2001 to December 2002.

The National Institute of Mental Health estimates that depression afflicts about 19 million adults in any given year.

Depression was more common in women and in adults 18-44 than in those over 60. The increase in people seeking treatment indicates raising awareness about depression are paying off.

Dr. William McKinney, a psychiatrist at Northwestern Memorial Hospital indicates a lot of people are unfortunately being put on some anti-depressant for an inadequate dose and perhaps for an inadequate time.

"More Being Treated for Depression, but Poorly, Study Says"
By Lindsey Tanner, AP, June, 2003

Treatments for major depression have Improved over the last 20 years, but still more than half are getting inadequate therapy. New findings suggest that even as the stigma of mental illness may be lessening, all doctors are not aware of treatment advances.

In a study of 9,090 people aged 18 and up, 57% of them had received treatment. Nearly 40% higher than in the 1980's. However in only 21% was treatments considered adequate. These findings published in the American Medical Association journal were based on evaluations from February 2001 to December, 2002. They estimate that depression afflicts 915 percent of adults—about 19 million in each year.

Depression was more common in women, and in adults aged 18-44 more than over 60.

Because of raised awareness about depression, more people are seeking treatment. Many people however are going to their doctors and being put on an anti-depressant for perhaps an inadequate dose for an inadequate time.

"Faith Community Reaches Out to Mentally Ill People"
By Maria Elena Baca

When a 20 year old man was hospitalized shortly after he was diagnosed with schizophrenia, he told his mother that he'd like to see his priest. When she called the rectory with this request, it was quickly asked if he was violent. This was someone who had always been thought of as a kind, neat young man. The question broke his mother's heart.

About the same time, his grandmother was diagnosed with cancer, and was immediately offered help from her faith community and friends. She stated that she had people from the church coming and offering help for everything, nothing for her son.

People didn't even ask how he was.

Fear, ignorance and shame prevent people from talking about Mental Illnesses even though they may affect as many as one in four Minnesota families.

This mother made a mission of educating congregations about mental illness and the needs of ill people and their families. She is charwoman of the Faithways program of the National Alliance for the Mentally Ill— offering training and other resources for religious communities.

Networks of groups, families and people who live with mental illnesses are trying to educate clergy and congregations to show them that persons with mental illness need their help and deserve their compassion.

Support is so needed—after the medical diagnosis, many times the church or synagogue is the first place people go for support. They need a sense of community.

Although leadership from clergy is key, the change often begins within the congregation.

If someone has experienced mental illness in their family will get their pastor or rabbi to form a group of people who really care about this issue it would perhaps be the break through that is really needed.

In 1986, Joanna Kuehn and a group of supporters founded the Task Force on Mental Illness/Brain Disorders at Mt. Olivet church in Minneapolis. The church sponsors a group home for people who live with severe and persistent mental illness. There is also a psychologist and a psychiatrist on the church staff. As she states, "This is part of our Christian faith bring that cup of cold water to someone who is in need."

"Hospital Stops Admitting Acute Psychiatric Patients"

In February, 2007 Immanuel St. Joseph's Hospital in Mankato Minnesota stopped providing inpatient care for acute psychiatric cases. They usually admit between 500 and 600 mental health patients annually. Only one-quarter of the state's 136 hospitals provide inpatient psychiatric care. Dr. Bill Rupp of ISJ Mayo Health said patients with less acute mental health problems will still be hospitalized.

Dr. Mark Matthias at the Mankato Clinic that provides care to the Hospitals patients, said the clinic went from six psychiatrists to three, and two of those remaining have additional duties elsewhere. Because of that, they have lost the ability to care for patients at the hospital.

If a person arrives in the Emergency department who needs hospitalization, they'll be taken to another hospital in the state. The loss of psychiatric beds will be a sad loss to the region.

"Army Sees Alarming Rise in Suicides"
By Dana Priest

Lt. Elizabeth Whiteside, a psychiatric outpatient at Walter Reed army Medical Center attempted to kill herself while awaiting a verdict on a pending court-martial.

She joined a record number of soldiers who have committed or tried to commit suicide after serving in the wars in Iraq or Afghanistan

Suicides among active-duty soldiers in 2007 reached their highest level since the Army began keeping records in 1980. In 2007 121 soldiers took their own lives. In 2007, about 2,100 soldiers injured themselves or attempted suicide, compared with about 350 in 2002.

The ongoing wars have placed severe stress on the Army. Historically, suicide rates usually decrease when soldiers are in conflicts overseas, but that has reversed. In 2001 the lowest rate on record, the suicide rate per 100,000 active duty soldiers was at 9.8%. In 2006 it reached an all-time high of 17.5%.

Col. Elspeth Cameron Ritchie, the Army's top psychiatrist states We need to improve our behavioral health care. It was found that common factors in suicides and attempted suicides include failed personal relationships; legal, financial or occupational problems; and frequency and length of overseas deployments.

The Army still does not know how to adequately assess, monitor and treat soldiers with psychological problems. The current Suicide Prevention Program was not designed for a combat/deployment environment.

"Senator Wants VA to Explain Events"

After an Iraq war veteran committed suicide, a U.S. senator from Hawaii,. Daniel Akaka,D has asked for an explanation from the Department of Veterans Affairs. His family had looked for help at two VA hospitals in Minnesota.

According to news reports, the soldier told a staff member at the VA hospital in St. Cloud two weeks before his suicide that he was thinking of killing himself and wanted to be admitted. He was told he couldn't be admitted that day. The next day he was told by phone that he was No. 26 on the waiting list. Four days later, he committed suicide.

A public affairs officer at the St. Cloud VA Medical Center said she couldn't comment on Akaka's letter and privacy laws prevented her from confirming if the young man had been at the facility. She expressed her sympathy to the family and friends, stating that they want to encourage anyone with suicidal thoughts to seek help.

A public affairs officer for the VA Medical Center in Minneapolis also could not get into specifics.

On January 16th, this young man called family and friends to tell them he was going to kill himself. They called local police who found he had hung himself.

It was stated that in 2004 many initiatives were developed to improve VA's ability to prevent suicide, but not all of those initiatives had been implemented

The Minnesota Senate issued a statement asking for information and urged the VA to find out what led to the tragedy.

"Mental Illness can Happen to Anyone"
By Beverly Brown

Mental illness doesn't discriminate. Whether you are a president, a writer, an artist or an astronaut. It has touched all of our lives in one way or another.

If you red a book by Ernest Hemingway or listed to music of Kurt Cobain, you've been touched by someone who had mental illness. If you know that Abraham Lincoln was a U.S. president and that Terry Bradshaw played for the Pittsburgh Steelers, you have known of someone with mental illness. The same with Maurice Benard on General Hospital and Greg Louganis in the 1988 Olympics. A long list of famous people whom we all would recognize have enriched our lives while living with a mental illness. If you have a family member or friend with a mental illness, you are not alone, as it affects one in five people.

They can be of any age, race, religion or socioeconomic status and affects the entire family.

Mental illness are treatable medical conditions. Schizophrenia, bipolar disorder, anxiety and many others can be helped. However, many people feel isolated due to the stigma and misinformation surrounding it, and can be overwhelming.

It was recently reported that ½ of the soldiers returning from Iraq will have some form of mental illness. Over 1 million have already served our country. When the war is over, will they be forgotten?

More soldiers that served in the Vietnam War have committed suicide than the number killed during the Vietnam War. We all need to be aware, and perhaps each of us can make a difference.

"Living with Bipolar Disorder"
By Dr. Tedd Mitchell

Even in the 1980s, medicines to treat bipolar disorder were few, but it has improved. Formerly called manic depression, this illness can be disruptive to a person's relationships, their jobs and even when taking care of oneself.

It is many times difficult to identify those who have it. When someone who has generally shown "normal" behavior acts irrationally, others often conclude that the person is behaving irresponsibly, but they may in fact need medical help.

A person with bipolar problems will have highs when they will seem unusually strong happiness, lots of energy, increased sex drives, easy distractibility and rapid speech. During this time, the person may shift from euphoria to irritability and have grandiose ideas, making poor decisions, perhaps such as large spending sprees.

Then come the "lows." The depressive phase displayed by feelings of loneliness, sadness and hopelessness. Yet, one doesn't always follow the other. People may develop a psychosis and find it impossible to deal with reality. Because of this, the possibility of suicide is a concern. Remember, medications are available, so talk with your doctor if you or a loved one have any symptoms that may be caused by this condition.

"Instead of Psychiatric Care, He Got Jail—For Half A Year"
By Kate Stanley

Gerald Lund spent 6 months in the St Louis County jail in MN. He hadn't been well for quite some time. The county sheriff's office know, as his worsening schizophrenia spurred them on to agree with family pleas that he be escorted to a hospital.

However, instead of bringing him to a hospital, they took him to jail. He was overlooked and untreated for more than half a year.

How did this happen? When the deputies picked him up, Gerald was carrying a gun. Psychiatrist Stephen Setterberg states that "Possession of a gun should in no way preclude hospitalization". It's evidence that treatment it needed. One shouldn't have to wait until a person gets dangerous.

Gerald's family were promised that they would take him to Miller Dwan Medical Center where a psych-ward bed was waiting. He had suffered with problems through his adult life, and when the thoughts were too much, he had ended up in the hospital where he got medicine to settle him down. Then he would return to live with his family on their farm where he helped to maintain farm machinery and take care of various animals. He even cooked and cleaned.

Late in September however, he walked into the bathroom to find his 94 year-old father dead, and it struck him extremely hard. Strange ideas arose in his head. When one of his sisters visited the farm, suddenly Gerald hurled her from an easy chair, shouting "You killed our father!"

That's when they asked the St. Louis County Sheriff's Dept. for help. It didn't happen, however as they didn't consider the chair toppling serious enough.

They then turned to the county's Social Services Department. She was told they couldn't help unless he was imminently dangerous to himself or others.

Apparently no one remembered that the Legislature changed the civil commitment law in 2001. Counties have been authorized to help families pursue commitment before danger is imminent. People with histories of psychiatric lapses often follow a predictable path towards peril.

"Spears Is Iill, Coverage of Her Is Sick"
By Asra Q. Nomani

I was just a teen when my brother was diagnosed with schiza-affective disorder, an illness that causes mood swings, psychosis and violent outbursts. Our family had committed him for psychiatric treatment. I wept, my parents sobbed, but at least we had privacy.

It's impossible to find any entertainment value in the harassment of Britney Spears when she was released from the psychiatric ward of UCLA.

Mental illness is hard to see, so it's hard to understand. All of us know that we wouldn't be so cruel to someone who had a brain tumor. Paparazzi and celebrity gossip Web sites are easy to blame. TMZ promoted a video of Spears crying over a photo of her sitting on a curb after a fight with her manager with "Britwreck" scrawled over it.

People magazine showed "Britney's Mental Illness" as one of their covers.

The Daily Telegraph's Web site stated "Mad Britney Spears detoxed by doctors. See pictures here. Even Barbara Walters reported on her mental health issues. Let's leave Britney and her family alone.

Journalists came to the ethical determination not to publish names of rape victims or to air gruesome terrorist videos. We can do the same here. Remember, Britney Spears is a 27 year old in a fight for her life.

"Crisis Line Goes Mobile"
By Renee Richardson

People having anxiety, depression and thoughts of suicide have had four options after regular business hours—gut it out or call a Crisis Line, Emergency Room or 911, but now, mobile mental health services have begun. It enables people to have an alternative to get in touch with trained mental health professionals when they may need them the most. A big step forward.

Statistically, Mark Bulitz at Northern Pines Mental Health Center said 25 percent of the population is dealing with some sort of mental health problem.

They received a grant to provide more immediate help for crisis services. They are in partnership with law enforcement, and emergency medical providers.

Crisis Line volunteers took extra training to handle mobile services. They welcomed the opportunity to be involved. Working with law enforcement officials and medical centers, they will contact the mobile crisis team.

Experienced team members will work in pairs and travel to the person in crises.

One of the team will be a licensed mental health professional and the other a mental health practitioner. They will asses what care is needed and connect the individual to those services. An area psychiatrist will be available should they be needed.

Credit for the mobile mental health services is shared with Region Five Plus Adult Mental Health Initiative, made up of representatives from six participating counties—Aitkin, Cass, Crow Wing, Morrison, Todd and Wadena. They have been working for years to try and get help for mental health services after regular business hours.

A very large step that has been so needed.

"House Favors Wellstone Bill to Expand
Health Coverage for Mental Health"
Washington (AP}

The House voted to require equal health insurance coverage for mental and physical illnesses when policies cover both.

The 268-138 roll call was cheered. Advocates have been fighting for over a decade to see this happen.

It is hoped that this would help end the stigma of mental illness and provide help for all those seeking it.

"The "Paul Wellstone Mental Health and Addiction Equity Act of 2007" is a historic step," said the late Senator Wellstone's son, David.

The House bill was sponsored by Reps. Patrick Kennedy, D-R.I., who has battled depression, alcoholism and drug abuse, and Jim Ramstad, R-Minn., a recovering alcoholic who is Kennedy's Alcoholic Anonymous sponsor" "It's about opening up the doors and ending the shadow of discrimination against the mentally ill," said Kennedy.

The younger Kennedy will negotiate with his father on a compromise measure.

Perhaps finally a break through (this came about in 2008).

"Scientists Try to Stop Schizophrenia in it's Tracks"

A young woman, now 21, who asked that her name not be used, recalled that she was happy in high school, but in college things changed. She became depressed and withdrawn, often not about to get out of bed. "I had really odd thoughts" while attending the University of Southern Maine. She felt like people were going to jump at her. Even though she knew it wasn't so, she still had fears. When she drove she saw shadowy imagined people. At times there would be a woman's voice she'd hear during class, or noises like knocking or a fizzy hiss in her ear.

She finally visited the school's health served and talked about feeling depressed. A nurse practitioner saw however, schizophrenia "prodrome"—

the early signs—involving a troubled mental state usually found in teens and young adults.

This prodrome can linger for weeks, or years before it gives way to psychosis—or it can mysteriously disappear without a trace.

Researchers are working on how to treat it. Now calling in tools like brain scans, DNA studies and hormone research they hope to find new ways to detect who's on the road to psychosis and stop the progression.

In the prodrome, people understand these experiences are just illusions. People with psychosis cling to unreasonable explanations instead.

After hearing the student's story, Ann Lovegren Conley, the family nurse practitioner at USM put her in touch with the Portland Identification and Early Referral program, called PIER—one of about 20 clinics in the United States.

PIER emphasizes non-drug therapies for its patients, ages 12 to 25 However, about three-quarters of them take anti-psychotic medication.

Dr. Thomas McGlashan, a Yale University psychiatry professor recalled that one young woman at the Yale clinic burst into tears when asked about symptoms, explained "I thought I was the only person in the world who was having these experiences.

Or when asked if they've felt like the television was speaking to them personally, clients may reply" How did you know?

When it comes to treating the prodrome, scientists say they have promising approaches, but no proven treatments to prevent psychosis from appearing.

Low doses of anti-psychotic drugs may help, but it's not clear if they can actually prevent psychosis. Side effects like serious weight gains are a problem. What's more the weight gain can turn young people away from the drugs, even if they become psychotic and clearly need them.

Perhaps finally recognizing signs and possible treatments? One can only hope so. Finally people are beginning to share "strange" things that seem to be happening to them. My daughter and I only hope that you will also find, through this book that if anything like this happens to you or to one you love, you are not alone, and there is help, so don't be overwhelmed and certainly not ashamed.

Chapter 14
Love, Faith and Hope for All

I was attending the University of Wisconsin when 2 months before Christmas break I started thinking new thoughts—profound ideas came to me. I felt powerful. Everything was great. I was doing well in my studies; I was popular and ready to meet any challenge.

Two weeks before Christmas break my mind became so clear it was as if God was speaking directly to me. Everything seemed to fall in place. I knew what people were going to say before they spoke. Gentle whispers came to me and I felt full of love for mankind. I thought I must have opened myself to the concepts of love and a God who works through us.

One week after Christmas break, the gentle whispers were becoming incessant and I couldn't quiet my mind. It was like having all of the radio stations in the world going through my mind and I had no control. I couldn't turn it off. Hundreds of thoughts would flash through my mind at once, instantly.

Now I wasn't sure if the voices came from God or from a demon who was trying to deceive me and pull me towards hell. Thus came about all of the episodes explained in this book.

Finding the right guidance was often difficult. Not every professional's methods were appropriate for my needs, thus requiring research, trial and error. There is no "set formula" of how to deal with any type of Mental Illness, as each person's reactions are different, and each person needs to be treated in various ways.

Society needs to be reminded of the vulnerability of the human psyche and the fact that none of us are immune to the possibility of mental illnesses. The stigma that is attached to those considered mentally ill is far too damaging.

The mentally ill have been shunned by society. Coming out of the dark ages took too long, and the inhuman treatments scarred too many. We must hope that society continues to make the steps ahead. We cannot just leave the advances that have only begun to come about so recently.

Finally I was ready to continue my progress back to self assurance and ready to continue my life. I finally find myself reaching the goals I had always wanted and I am able to meet every challenge along the way and forge through it and continue to reach.

Thankfully I had Love surrounding me at all times. I had Faith in God and Faith in the people who love me. This all gave me Hope that I could find my way back to the life I wanted. For all of you readers who may be searching for answers for yourself or some loved one, I sincerely hope that what you have read may encourage you to believe that with work, determination, and finding the right help, your path will go well and God will lead you and be at your side as you are victorious over the illness.

The first 2-3 years after Laurie's breakdown were difficult for all of us. It certainly wasn't a completely smooth road. There were many strides forward, but also slips backwards, but with Laurie's perseverance and all of our family giving patient, ongoing support, we proved that love of one another and a strong faith in God can make good things conquer over bad.

As time went on, Laurie continued to grow emotionally—not just "back to normal" but becoming stronger than ever before. Our confidence in her grew to surpass any hopes and dreams we may have had for her to become a capable, responsible adult.

Laurie is admired and respected by those who come to know her. She is an avid worker for the church in many areas, and is becoming a strong leader, but is always a good listener and ready to accept other peoples suggestions.

She forged through her emotional problems, even enduring many of the "usual" stresses of this age—marriage, divorce, job situations, buying and maintaining her own home, making new relationships, and while handling all of these, has continued to be a stable, capable person. By living through her ordeal, she gained much understanding and compassion which she shows towards everyone.

Laurie is reaching middle age now, and is a beautiful person, both in appearance and in personality. Since we went through her breakdown many years ago, I'm pleased to report that some aspects of mental health have shown improvement. There are now help lines available, new books and articles giving knowledge to the illness, etc. However, many sides of mental health issues have found few changes. Most people can confront and show compassion to persons with cancer or AIDS, but confronting and comforting a person with emotional problems is still a dilemma to most. No one is ashamed to have a family member who has cancer, and no one should ever be ashamed to have a family member who has a mental breakdown. They are no less intelligent, no less frightened and no less feeling a need to be loved and understood.

It takes a lot of work to overcome this completely unexplained illness. No one has as yet found out exactly what causes it, and no single way to treat it. Many cases may have similarities, but as each person is different, each case is different also. X-Rays, MRI's, Ultrasounds or blood tests reveal little of this illness, only interrupted brain waves that somehow bring on strange behavior and thoughts make it evident. We have a long way to go in finding answers to what brings on these changes and why some people are affected and others are not.

Laurie and I only want to let you know that roads do continue on beyond this illness. If you are going through this with anyone you love, once the fight back to reality has begun and been attained, there are still many hurdles to go over, but don't give up. Some run the race faster, and some more slowly, but the finish line may be ahead. Just remember that the person going through this needs you to hold their hand, sometimes pulling, sometimes guiding, but always touching and giving love squeezes when needed.

As Laurie has become an adult, our relationship has cemented, changing only to our becoming best of friends—sharing thoughts, secrets, laughter, and always love.

I trust her wholly to aim for whatever she wants, work hard for it and attain it. She is Strong!! She is Invincible!! She is my darling daughter.

Bibliography

Autio, Sharon. "Mental Illness is no laughing matter." *Mille Lacs Messenger* (Isle, MN) July 6, 2000

Baca, Maria Elena. "Faith community reaches out to mentally ill people." *Minneapolis Star Tribune*, July 12, 2005 Faith and Values Section B6 & 7

Befrienders. "Befrienders Worldwide" 2009 http://who.int/mental_health

Bregin, Peter. *Toxic Psychiatry*. St. Martins Press, 1991.

Brown, Beverly "Mental illness can happen to anyone" *Brainerd Dispatch* (Brainerd, MN)—Guest Column, 2008

Delay and Denikar, two pioneers of the drug Thorazine in 1952

"Dr. Walter Freeman—Lobotomies" *Public Television Documentary* aired on PBS in January of 2008 Farmer, Frances. "This is Frances Farmer." http://www.francesfarmersrevenge.com

Foreman, Judy."New tool in treating mental disorders." *Minneapolis Star Tribune,* June 16, 2003 Health Section

Goulston, Mark S. "Stigma—Our Social Virus." *Los Angeles Times,* May 8, 1989

Goulston, Mark S. LA Times "Have a look in your own mirror for a glimpse of mental illness." *Minneapolis Star Tribune,*" July, 1990 Sunday Editorial Section

"Hospital stops admitting acute psychiatric patients." Brainerd Dispatch (Brainerd, MN) Feb. 2007

"House favors Wellstone bill to expand health coverage for mental health" *Brainerd Dispatch,* (Brainerd, MN) March, 2008

Hughes, Richard and Robert Brewin *Tranquilizing of America.* 1979

Kaye, Randi "Private Wounds." *Minnesota Monthly* May, 2003:45-54 "(page 53)"

"Warning Signs of Suicide " *San Francisco Suicide Prevention and Befrienders International,* "(Kaye 54)"

"Live Your Life Well" *MHA* 2009 http://www.mentalhealthamerica.net "Mental Health: Types of Mental Illness." Webmd 27 Sept. 2009 http://www.webmd.com/mental-health

Mitchell, Tedd, M.D. "Living with bipolar disorder" *"USA Weekend"* Feb. 8-10, 2008

Health Smart "page 14"

Nomani, Asra Q. special to LA times "Spears is ill; coverage of her is sick" *Brainerd Dispatch* (Brainerd, MN) February, 2008

Priest, Dana, Wash. Post "Army sees alarming rise in suicides" *Brainerd Dispatch* (Brainerd, MN) Jan. 2007

Richardson, Renee "Crisis Line Goes Mobile" *Brainerd Dispatch* 2008

"Scientists try to stop schizophrenia in its tracks." *Brainerd Dispatch"* (Brainerd, MN) July, 2009

"Senator wants VA to explain events before the suicide", *Brainerd Dispatch* (Brainerd, MN) 1 Feb. 2007

Stanley, Kate "Instead of psychiatric care, he got jail—for half a year" *Brainerd Dispatch,* (Brainerd, MN) 2008

Tanner, Lindsey.—AP "More being treated for depression, but poorly, study says." *Minneapolis Star Tribune,* June 18, 2003 Health Section.

"What Is Depression." webmd 27 Sept. 2009 http://www.webmd.com/depression.guide

World Health Orginazation 2009 http://who.int/mental_health